The night was alive – a thousand times more alive than you could possibly imagine when you were at home, tucked up in your warm, cosy bed! And the night had thousands of eyes – eyes that remained invisible to Tony. But they were watching him, because they could see in the dark …

Tony felt his hair beginning to stand on end. He looked over once more at the entrance hole and, as though his words could conjure them up, he spoke aloud, urgently but softly, "Rudolph, Anna, I'm here!"

Follow the spooky adventures of Tony and his vampire friends in this new series of *The Little Vampire* books:

The Little Vampire in Danger
The Little Vampire in the Vale of Doom
The Little Vampire in Despair
The Little Vampire and the Mystery Patient
The Little Vampire in the Lion's Den
The Little Vampire Learns to be Brave
The Little Vampire Gets a Surprise
The Little Vampire and the Wicked Plot
The Little Vampire and the School Trip

Angela Sommer-Bodenburg

the little Vampire AND THE SCHOOL TRIP

Illustrated by Anthony Lewis

Translated by Sarah Gibson

SIMON & SCHUSTER
YOUNG BOOKS

This book is for Burghardt Bodenburg, who is now the proud possessor of two pairs of vampire teeth; and also for everyone like me, who knows how much fun – but also just how alarming – a school trip can be.

First published in Germany in 1990 by C. Bertelsmann Verlag GmbH

First published in Great Britain in 1994
by Simon & Schuster Young Books
Campus 400
Maylands Avenue
Hemel Hempstead
Herts HP2 7EZ

Set in 12pt Goudy Old Style by
Derek Doyle & Associates, Mold, Clwyd
Printed and bound by the
Guernsey Press Co Ltd, Channel Islands

British Library Cataloguing in Publication Data available

ISBN 0 7500 1537 3
ISBN 0 7500 1538 1 (pb)

Contents

The story so far...

Tony's best friends – Rudolph and Anna Sackville-Bagg – are vampires! They live with their creepy Aunt Dorothy and their teenage brother, Greg, in the family vault in the cemetery.

Anna and Tony are in love with each other, which sometimes makes Rudolph very jealous! Rudolph is in love with Olga Pigsbubble, a spoilt, selfish vampire who Tony and Anna can't stand! Luckily, she has gone away, but Rudolph still yearns after her.

The vampires' enemies are McRookery and his assistant Sniveller, who are the nightwatchmen at the cemetery where the vampires live. Recently the vampires were almost caught out by a ruthless vampire-hunter called Professor Careless who disguised himself as a vampire by the name of Igno von Rant.

Are You Packing?

"Suddenly something rustled in the undergrowth . . ." said the deep voice on Tony's radio.

Tony was busy packing his rucksack. He stopped and looked at the radio, eager to hear what was about to happen in the story.

"Then a figure stepped out of the shadows of the tall trees," continued the storyteller's voice. "It was a man dressed in black, and in his hand he was carrying – a club!"

At that precise moment, something knocked on Tony's windowpane and he screamed. Then he glanced across at the window and flushed. The figure dressed in black who was trying to reach *him* wasn't carrying a club. No, and what's more she was smiling!

Tony quickly switched off the radio. He ran over to the window and opened it. There outside sat Anna, looking at him tenderly. "May I come in?" she asked.

"Yes, of course," he replied, clearing his throat in embarrassment. He was sure Anna must have seen him jump! And his scream probably hadn't escaped her, either. Vampires have very good ears! And good eyes too – Anna was studying the rucksack in surprise. "Are you packing?" she asked.

"Yeah, worse luck."

"But I thought your school trip had been cancelled!"

"I thought so too."

"Didn't you say your teacher was ill?" asked Anna.

"Yes, she is," Tony said. "But our maths teacher, Mr Flyswotter, has stepped in."

"Stepped in what?"

"Mr Flyswotter's coming instead of our teacher. He hasn't got a class of his own, and that's why he's taking us to Crumbletomb."

The corners of Anna's mouth twitched. "That's rotten!"

Tony nodded glumly. "The school trip will be even more deadly with old Flyswotter."

"Can't you do anything to stop it? All go on strike, or something?"

"No, nothing. The rooms in the youth hostel are reserved, the coach is booked . . . ."

"The coach?" Anna's eyes began to gleam. "Are you going on a coach? Coaches have huge luggage compartments, don't they?"

Tony could guess what she was wondering: whether she could fit her coffin in and have it taken along as well. But it was a vain hope. "We're leaving tomorrow morning," he explained. "At half past nine."

"Are you travelling during the day?" inquired Anna, disappointed.

He nodded. "The trip only lasts from Monday till Friday. And Mr Flyswotter's organized a jam-packed programme for us. As soon as we've unpacked our things, he wants to set off on a walk!"

"Huh, how boring!" snorted Anna.

Tony pulled his new ankle boots out from under the bed.

"Here, I've got these especially for all the walking. They're about the only good thing about the whole trip!"

Anna made her hands into fists. "I'd come with you on

your school trip! But Rudolph wouldn't help me get my coffin over to Crumbletomb."

"What if you begged him?"

"No." Anna shook her head. "Ever since Olga and Aunt Dorothy went away, you can't have a sensible conversation with Rudolph. And Greg wouldn't help me, either! Every night he goes off to his Men's Music Group – huh! And my parents and grandparents have got much more suspicious since Aunt Dorothy's engagement fell through," she added. "Now I have to tell them exactly why I'm going out, where I'm going and who I'm going to see."

Anna sniffed. "Nothing every goes right for us – nothing!"

Disconcerted, Tony set about trying to fasten his rucksack. Anna was right, of course – the vampires' existence really was fraught with difficulties. Dangers threatened them from all sides – nightwatchmen in the cemetery, vampire hunters . . . and lately, vampire researchers like Professor Careless. Under the false name of Igno von Rant, he had attempted to marry into the Sackville-Bagg family so that he could follow up his research at first hand.

"I shall come and visit you," declared Anna with a determined expression.

"That won't be easy," Tony pointed out. "In the youth hostel, we're under supervision the whole time. And we all have to sleep in dormitories."

"Dormitories?" repeated Anna, taken aback. "Do you mean . . . with *girls?*"

Tony stifled a smile. "No. The girls are sleeping up in the attic rooms, and we boys are on the ground floor."

"Thanks be to Dracula!" Anna sighed. "Do you feel like doing anything?" she asked after a pause, looking at him expectantly.

"Doing something?" Tony hesitated. His mother had announced that she would like to go through the contents of his rucksack one more time with him. "Yes, I do, but —"

A shadow flickered over Anna's face. "But you're already thinking about all the girls in your class, aren't you?"

"No, why d'you say that?" he asked indignantly.

"Because you had such a faraway look on your face! And because you still haven't noticed that I put on some 'Fragrance of Eternal Love' especially for you!"

"I *had* noticed!" he contradicted her.

"Then why didn't you say anything about it?" asked Anna sulkily.

"I hadn't got round to it," Tony explained. He would never have a chance to now, because just then, he heard footsteps in the hall.

"Mum!" he whispered.

Anna climbed nimbly on to the window-sill.

"Is there only one youth hostel in Crumbletomb?" she asked.

"Yes. The road's called Quiet Forest Way."

"Quiet Forest Way?" Anna giggled. "Well, see you soon, Tony!"

"When?" he asked.

"Tomorrow, I hope," she answered, flying out into the night. At that moment, Tony's mother came into the room.

"Aren't you ready yet?" she asked.

"No, how can I be," he grumbled, "if you keep on wanting to rummage through everything again?"

"It's for your own good," she replied. "I just don't want you to be one of those boys who always go away without the most important things!"

"I'm already one of them," growled Tony. It was true: the most important things for him were his vampire friends!

Poisonous Fangs

Of course Tony did have a couple of other friends in his class. During the coach journey they talked about table tennis, bike rides and girls.

Tony crouched low in his seat, feeling rather fed up.

"What do *you* think of the new girl then?" asked Olly, who was sitting next to him.

"What should I think of her?" he growled.

"Well, *I* think she looks great!" Olly whispered.

Now Tony had to grin. This was an Olly he hadn't known before! But the new girl – she was called Viola and had only been in the class a week – was very pretty, with her long blonde hair, big blue eyes and little turned-up nose.

What disturbed Tony, though, was how much she looked like the Honourable Olga Pigsbubble, the great love of the Little Vampire's life. Viola seemed to be just as conceited and selfish as Olga, too.

"We must get a disco evening going as soon as we get to the youth hostel," suggested Henry. He was sitting in the row behind Olly and Tony. "I bet that new girl can dance just as good as she looks!"

"A disco evening?" repeated Tony doubtfully. "With Mr Flyswotter? I bet you it'll be more like an evening's walk!"

But they were in for a walk even before they'd had lunch! Tony and the others hardly had time to unpack their things into the narrow cupboards and make up their beds. They were bunk beds, and there were three of them in Tony's room.

Mrs Tallhat and Mrs Nutcake, two mothers who had come along to support Mr Flyswotter, helped them with their beds. Even so, it seemed to take forever. Tony was still toiling with the heavy old woollen blanket, which had CRUMBLETOMB FRESH AIR HOSTEL stamped on it, when Mr Flyswotter came in, and told them to hurry up. They must get a move on and take a look at the beautiful surroundings they found themselves in. "Beautiful surroundings . . ." In Tony's opinion, it was a really boring bit of countryside. Hills here, hills there, and round every corner there was the same landscape: another hill, trees, bushes, heather.

"Are there any snakes round here, Mr Flyswotter?" asked Sebastian.

"I expect you're talking about poisonous snakes!" Mr Flyswotter answered.

A couple of the children screamed, and Viola yelped the loudest.

"All you'll find here are slow-worms," Mr Flyswotter assured them, "and they haven't got poisonous fangs."

"I want to go home!" wailed Viola.

"If you keep to the paths, nothing will happen," answered Mrs Nutcake.

"Exactly!" Mr Flyswotter agreed. "In any case, you are *forbidden* to wander off the paths."

A lot of other things were forbidden too, Tony thought to himself after lunch (which, to his astonishment, had been delicious: chicken soup and vanilla pudding with raspberry sauce).

Afterwards, the man in charge – whose name was, appropriately, Mr Dredfel – gave them a long lecture about all the things that were forbidden in his hostel.

"It's going to be difficult to find anything we *can* do!" whispered Olly to Tony.

"Don't worry," Tony replied sarcastically. "We'll be allowed to go to bed at six o'clock and turn out our lights straight away, and we'll be allowed to help with the washing-up in the kitchen, and peel potatoes, but no running, no shouting, no music . . ."

Tony and Olly were immediately given a bad mark by Mr Flyswotter for being cheeky. As a punishment, they were made to clear away all the dishes.

"I'd rather clear off from here than clear away all this!" sighed Olly.

"Clear off?" Tony grinned. "Just watch how many plates you carry at once. If you break any, you'll be cleared out of pocket money to buy some new ones!"

Olly groaned. "Please, not that! I've only got a fiver to keep me going this week!"

"I don't think there'll be much to spend it on," Tony told him. "The nearest shop's at least three miles away."

Tony at least had something else to keep him going: the thought that Anna just might come and visit him – might even come *tonight*! He had brought his vampire cloak – or rather, Uncle Theodore's vampire cloak – with him, just in case.

Corns and Blisters

In the afternoon, Mr Flyswotter wanted to climb Barren Head, a mountain that was "only" an hour's walk away.

But Mary and Pedro, the spokeschildren for the class, managed to persuade Mrs Tallhat and Mrs Nutcake that *one* walk was enough for the day. The two mothers, in their turn, managed to dissuade Mr Flyswotter from his ambitious plans – at least for that day.

"I think he wants to get us into the *Guinness Book of Records*" remarked Tanya.

"I don't think even we could walk enough kilometres to get into that," retorted Sebastian.

"No, I'm not talking about kilometres," said Tanya. "I mean the record number of corns and blisters we get on this holiday!"

Instead of going for a walk, they played games. After supper – rose-hip tea and porridge, which didn't appeal to anyone except Mr Flyswotter, who went back for three helpings – they had "free time". But there wasn't much to do with their free time, here in 'Quiet Forest Way'!

"Did you ever ask Mr Flyswotter if we could have a disco?" Olly asked Henry.

"Yeah, 'course I did," answered Henry.

"And?"

"He said if we do, it'll be on the last evening."

"On the last evening?" echoed Olly in dismay. "Huh! We'll have died of boredom by then."

Tony grinned to himself. He would make sure *he* had some fun – after all, he would have Anna! But first he would somehow have to leave his room unnoticed and meet her outside. Would she really come this evening? Anyway, it would be convenient if everybody – his school friends, Mr Flyswotter and the two mums – went to sleep as early as possible, he thought. The best thing would be to lead the way and set a good example . . .

And so it was that Tony was already in bed by half past nine. He explained to his room-mates that it was for Mr Flyswotter's benefit – surely he would be more willing to agree to the disco, and would give his permission sooner, if all was quiet in the evenings?

This tempting prospect persuaded them all to turn out the lights at a quarter to ten, and conversations continued in whispers. It wasn't long before whispering made them tired and everyone was asleep – except Tony.

He lay under his blanket, waiting till all was quiet in the other rooms too. But doors kept closing, and someone went running to the bathroom, giggling. In fact, the noise began to increase. Doors were slammed with more of a bang, and the laughter and talking grew louder and louder.

At last Mr Flyswotter put in an appearance. Tony recognized his energetic footsteps coming along the passage, and then he began to bellow: "If this racket does not stop immediately, we shall all go for a twenty-mile hike tomorrow! And twenty-five miles the day after! And thirty miles on Thursday! Then we'll see if anyone still has the energy for all this mucking about!"

Suddenly there was silence. In fact, it was almost too quiet, Tony thought. Mr Flyswotter's threat had obviously worked. Tony could still hear the odd giggle, and a couple of times someone slipped hurriedly down the passage. But apart from that, all was quiet. Finally – Tony looked at his watch and saw it was already eleven o'clock – it seemed that everyone had gone to sleep.

No, one person was still awake!

Tony stood up, pulled on his tracksuit and went over to the door. He opened it cautiously. It creaked, just as he had expected it would. But nothing happened.

He tiptoed down the passage to the dining room, where he opened a window and climbed out. The cool night air closed round him, and somewhere quite close, an owl hooted.

Or was it a real owl? All at once, Tony's heart was in his mouth. How could he be sure that it was Anna waiting for him, and not one of the others? After all, she had said that her parents and grandparents had become far more suspicious. What if one of the grown-up vampires had followed her . . . ?

But Anna would have noticed someone following her, Tony thought to himself, and if that were the case, she wouldn't have flown straight to the youth hostel.

It must have been an owl. Tony peered curiously over to the huge old tree growing in front of the building. There it was: he could make out a large black bird crouching on one of the branches, staring back at him. It must be a giant owl! he thought.

Then suddenly he realized it wasn't an owl at all. It was . . . a vampire!

What a Coincidence!

"Anna?" he called cautiously.

There was a soft laugh, and a merry voice answered, "Good evening, Tony!"

Once more, his heart was in his mouth, but this time with relief and excitement.

Then, "Hallo, Tony!" came a second, deeper voice.

Now Tony could see another figure next to Anna, dressed all in black.

"Rudolph, is that you?" he asked, half pleased, half in disbelief.

"Nice surprise, hey?" said the Little Vampire. "Yeah, I wanted to find out if school trips were really as exciting as Anna made out."

"Exciting? There's hardly anything more boring!" retorted Tony.

"Try as I might, I don't see how you can call that pretty blonde girl boring!" The Little Vampire giggled and pointed to the top floor windows. "If only she hadn't drawn the curtains . . ."

"The pretty blonde girl?" said Tony, puzzled.

"Rudolph thinks she looks like Olga," Anna revealed.

"Oh, no . . ." Tony groaned softly. They could only be talking about Viola!

"That's not true!" hissed the Little Vampire. "No one could look like Olga!

"But she's the same type as Olga," the vampire

continued in an enthusiastic tone of voice. "And she cares about her appearance, too."

"What do you mean?" asked Tony.

"She took at least half an hour to brush her hair," Anna informed him.

"With a pink hairbrush," added the Little Vampire with a sigh. "Tell you what, Tony," he blurted out, "couldn't you arrange a rendezvous?"

"A what?"

"A meeting," the Little Vampire repeated, swinging himself down from the tree. "Tomorrow evening, say, just after sunset."

"Who with?" Tony pretended not to understand.

"Who with? *Who with?*" snorted the Little Vampire. "With the pretty blonde girl, of course! Or are *you* interested in her yourself?" he asked suspiciously, after a pause.

"Yes, *I'd* like to know that, too!" cried Anna, landing in front of Tony with a dark look on her face. "You like girls with long, blonde hair, don't you?" she demanded.

"I don't care about the colour of their hair!" retorted Tony. "I like girls who are *nice*, like you!"

"Really?" Anna sniffed tearfully.

"And I'm definitely not interested in Viola!" declared Tony firmly.

"Viola? Is that her name?" demanded the Little Vampire.

"Yes."

"Viola . . . The second great love of Count Dracula had the same name: Viola the Reserved," murmured the Little Vampire thoughtfully.

Tony grinned. "The *second* great love?" he said. "What a coincidence!"

"What do you mean, coincidence?" asked the Little

Vampire coldly.

"Well . . . the similarities between you and Count Dracula . . ."

"You're right!" The Little Vampire gave a self-satisfied laugh. "So we're agreed on that?"

"Agreed?"

"Yes. Tomorrow, just after sunset, I'll be waiting for you and Viola." He giggled. "Over there, on the edge of the forest," he finished pompously.

"But —" Tony began. But the Little Vampire had already spread out his arms under his cloak.

"I'm relying on you," he said in a deep, hollow voice. "Now I *must* go and do something about these terrible hunger pangs in my tummy!"

With that, he rose into the air and flew quickly away.

Blacker than Black

"What a friend!" said Tony furiously to Anna.

"I'm just pleased that he came along at all," Anna announced. "Just lately he hasn't felt like doing anything. Our grandmother, Sabina the Sinister, says Rudolph has sunk into a mental depression."

"Mental depression?" repeated Tony. That certainly sounded very worrying!

Anna nodded. "He sees everything as blacker than black. But you can't help feeling sorry for him. First of all, there was that course of treatment with the psychologist, which he'd set such hopes by. In the end, it was all just a swindle. . ."

"Swindle?" asked Tony indignantly. "It was an experiment, a scientific experiment," he corrected her. "Mr Crustscrubber never *promised* he could cure Rudolph of his fear of sunlight."

"Whether he promised or not, Rudolph believed in the treatment," replied Anna. "If you believe in something, and then you're let down, it's like falling into a deep, dark hole, my grandmother says."

Tony gave a start. "Your grandmother said that? Does she know that Rudolph was on a course of treatment with Mr Crustscrubber?"

"No, whatever are you thinking of?" Anna reassured him. "In any case, Rudolph wasn't only let down by Mr Crustscrubber. A whole heap of things happened at the same time: the disappointment over the psychologist, the truth about Igno von Rant, the fact that Olga went flying off with Aunt Dorothy . . . and above all, Olga liking Hugo the Hairy better than him!"

"Did she say that?"

"No. Wally the Wicked told us. Olga didn't even bother to say goodbye to Rudolph."

"Didn't she?"

"I suppose she managed to say goodbye to *you*!" said Anna grimly.

"She never came to my house," Tony assured her, adding, "luckily!"

Anna smiled in relief. "Because he's sunk into this mental depression, I was actually quite pleased that Rudolph wanted to come this evening," she went on. "And then Viola . . . You must try all you can to get her to come to the rendezvous tomorrow evening."

"Do you really mean I can try *anything*?" said Tony with a grin.

Anna blushed. "I mean, you must persuade her! You know very well how to do that!"

"But I won't enjoy doing it," Tony said ruefully.

"Why ever not?" asked Anna.

"Because Viola isn't my type!"

"Oh, Tony!" Anna looked at him with a secret smile. "How sweet of you to say that!"

Tony cleared his throat. "Did you have any problems finding the youth hostel?" he asked, quickly changing the subject.

"No, it was quite easy."

"What about your relations?"

"I told them I wanted to concoct a new perfume, 'Fragrance of Irresistible Desire', that I needed some very rare herbs for it and that I'd have to fly a long way to find them. And I also told them Rudolph would be coming with me, to get his mind on something else."

"How did you persuade Rudolph to come with you?"

"Oh, I just told him there was a fantastic girl in your class, and that while you were on the school trip, he'd have his one and only chance of meeting her."

"But how did you know?" Tony asked, puzzled.

"I didn't!" Anna giggled. "I just made up the bit about the girl to get Rudolph going. Otherwise he'd never have budged from his coffin. At first, he wasn't in the slightest bit interested – because he wasn't going to be unfaithful to Olga, just imagine! But then I explained to him that he absolutely *had* to make Olga jealous if he wanted to outshine Hugo the Hairy. And that's what finally persuaded him."

Anna rubbed her hands together, looking pleased with herself. "And now there's this unbelievable coincidence – or stroke of luck, rather – here in the youth hostel! A girl who looks as though she could be Olga's sister! Rudolph couldn't believe it at first. Neither could I, for that matter!"

Anna gave a loud chuckle. "Dracula must have fixed it up, or that's what my mother, Thelma the Thirsty, would have said!"

"Dracula must have fixed it up?" Tony felt a cold shudder run down his spine. After all, not only was he going to have to persuade Viola to come and meet a total stranger – that stranger was also . . . a vampire!

"I must fly now," said Anna, breaking into his thoughts.

Tony pulled himself together. "So soon?"

"It's going to take me quite a long time to find all these rare herbs." Anna pulled a black pouch out from under her cloak. "If this isn't full to the brim, my parents and grandparents are going to get suspicious – and anyway, there'll be more time tomorrow evening," she added softly.

"Are you coming back tomorrow?" asked Tony.

"Of course!" she replied. "All you have to do is introduce the pair of them. After that, Rudolph certainly won't want you hanging around. Then you and I can go off and do something together."

"Hmm, I see." Yet again, Tony had an uncomfortable feeling about what the Little Vampire was planning for his rendezvous with Viola.

But Anna would be around too, he remembered. And in any case, he wasn't at all sure how he was going to persuade Viola to come and meet Rudolph in the first place.

"See you tomorrow then," said Anna gently.

"Yeah, see you," he replied.

Anna waved her arms and flew away.

Tony watched until the dark night had swallowed her up. Then he climbed back through the window into the dining room.

He got back to his room without bumping into anybody, took off his tracksuit and crept under the blankets. In the bed next to him, Olly was snoring loudly. But Tony was so tired that he fell asleep almost at once.

Devil's Rocks

The next morning, Mr Flyswotter announced a walk to Devil's Rocks.

Because the name sounded promising, only a few people in Tony's class grumbled. Tony wasn't one of them. He had decided to use the walk as a way of getting into conversation with Viola.

He had already made a plan by breakfast time. Whatever else happened, he was determined to be different from the boys who seemed to cluster permanently around Viola, gazing at her with open admiration. They were treated fairly cuttingly by her, just as Olga had behaved towards the Little Vampire. Tony wanted to be near her, but he decided he would deliberately "ignore" her. It might prick her curiosity and her vanity, because Viola couldn't stand it when a boy took absolutely no notice of her at all!

His plan seemed to work. As Tony walked along beside her, pretending she wasn't there, Viola kept glancing over at him.

Finally she spoke to him. "Are you new in class as well?"

"No, why?" he answered.

"Because you're so shy!" Henry interrupted, giggling. He spent the whole time making stupid jokes and then laughing louder than anyone.

"I'm not shy," Tony said with dignity. "But your

idiotic jokes are getting on my nerves."

"Mine too," said Viola.

"I suppose you're a bit older than the others," she said after a pause.

"Older?" repeated Tony.

"Yes. You're so quiet and serious." She looked around. "All the others here are really childish, but you —"

Tony had to bite his tongue to stop himself from laughing.

"You're called Tony, aren't you?" Viola said.

He nodded. She giggled in an affected way. Then she turned to her friend Sonia and began to whisper to her.

Tony walked on, apparently unruffled. He was sure that he was over the first hurdle. He had aroused Viola's interest. Everything else would turn out all right.

At Devil's Rocks, which didn't look in the least bit "devilish", but were heaps of ordinary grey boulders, Tony sat down on a rock a couple of metres away from Viola and unpacked his second breakfast.

Now and then he looked over at her. She was surrounded by eight boys and seemed to be incredibly bored by them – especially Henry, who was distinguishing himself again with his dreadful jokes.

Suddenly Viola stood up and came over to Tony.

"Some boys are just a pain in the neck," she groaned, sitting down next to him. "And the worst ones are the ones who don't seem to realize it."

Tony grinned.

"What about you?" asked Viola. "Do you always sit on your own?"

"No," he replied. "But I don't think much of always pretending to be sociable."

"I don't either!" Viola sighed. "I hate school trips more than anything else. Everything's so primitive: the dormitories, the wash rooms . . ." She plucked at a strand of blonde hair. "Yesterday I had to wash my hair in freezing cold water!"

"Really?" was all Tony said.

"You're not very talkative, are you?" she remarked, wrinkling her eyebrows as she looked at him.

"Can't you see we're being watched?" countered Tony.

Viola's mouth twitched. "Yes, by that boring lot over there! But I don't care two hoots about them and their stupid jokes!"

"No, I wasn't talking about them." Tony found it hard to stay serious. It had suddenly occurred to him how he could arouse Viola's interest even more. The magic word was – jealousy! "Tanya," he whispered. "She's looking at us!"

"Tanya?" said Viola in surprise.

"Sssh!" Tony put a finger to his lips. "She mustn't realize we're talking about her."

"Why not?"

"Because then she'll get really jealous!"

"Jealous? Is Tanya your girlfriend then?"

"Well . . . not exactly."

"What do you mean, not exactly?"

"Because I'm going to finish with her today. This evening, after supper," Tony told her.

"Really?" Viola giggled. "Do you think you might be getting interested in a *different* girlfriend?"

Tony just managed to stop himself from laughing. He knew, of course, which "different" girlfriend Viola was thinking of: herself!

"Could be," he said, deliberately vague, and then added, "Anyway, come out into the yard this evening, when it's dark. Then all will be revealed!"

"When it's dark?" Viola seemed excited by this

suggestion. "Will you have finished with Tanya by then?" she asked, glancing across at the other girl in spite of what Tony had said. Tony could see a look of triumph on her face.

"Yes, of course," he said.

Viola gave a little flirtatious giggle. "All right then," she whispered. "See you this evening." She stood up and went back to sit with her circle of admirers, the picture of innocence.

Tony watched her contentedly. It certainly wasn't a "devilish" plan he had cooked up here on Devil's Rocks, but even so, everything had worked out so well that he could almost believe some sort of "devilish" power must have been helping him!

Probably just the power of love! he thought to himself, grinning.

On the walk home, everybody grumbled that the Devil's Rocks had been a great disappointment, and they could have done without the walk to get there.

" – and without the blisters, too!" added Melanie.

Tony, on the other hand, was feeling decidedly chirpy; probably because he had managed to get Viola to agree to meet him that evening!

However, his good mood vanished when they got back to the hostel and were made to write letters home. And that wasn't all: afterwards, Mr Flyswotter handed out exercise books and announced that from now on, everyone had to keep a diary.

"Why do we have to do that?" cried Olly.

"I'm not having you running about the place like headless chickens any more. I want you to start using your eyes to see the lovely things around us," answered Mr Flyswotter.

"Lovely things?" Henry giggled, holding a hand in

front of his mouth. "My eyes certainly haven't missed *one* lovely thing, tee hee!"

"I want you to write at least two pages every day," went on Mr Flyswotter. "And a few drawings will get you even better marks."

"Are you going to mark them?" asked Stephen indignantly.

"Of course," Mr Flyswotter told him. "Or did you think you were here just to enjoy yourselves?"

"Yes, I did," grumbled Stephen.

So it was that they all had to sit in the dining room, heads bent over exercise books, just as if they were at school.

Tony gave a sigh and began describing the first two days – leaving out his night-time visit from Anna and Rudolph, of course. Nor did he mention his arrangement with Viola for this evening.

After quite a long time, he'd managed to cover two pages in his biggest handwriting. He stood up and went out into the yard with the others who had finished before him.

"Diaries, letters home . . . it's psychological torture!" Sebastian was complaining.

Tony grinned. "No it's not. It's just an ordinary school trip!"

"We won't put up with it," remarked Olly. "We ought to suggest some different things, like night walks, a paperchase, camp fires, or a disco evening . . . And then we must get Mrs Tallhat and Mrs Nutcake on our side."

"Of course there's no harm in making suggestions like that," said Tony rather pessimistically. "But I doubt whether they'll do any good with old Flyswotter."

Tony's misgivings turned out to be all too true. On the subject of night walks, Mr Flyswotter said that they would be far too dangerous: what if someone fell into a bog or down a hole? The paperchase was no good either. "Thousands of innocent beetles would be trampled to death!" he said.

He didn't rule out a camp fire or a disco for the last evening – just so long as the rest of the days went by "without any unfortunate mishaps".

"The biggest unfortunate mishap is old Flyswotter himself!" declared Sebastian through clenched teeth.

"I wish I could just pack my bags and go," grumbled Olly.

Tony wasn't so gloomy. After all, "Every horrible day has a happy ending," he declared.

Gazing into Space

The evening didn't get off to a particularly good start. Everyone was sitting around in the dining room, feeling cross. Some people were still writing in their diaries, or doing drawings to earn extra marks. Others were playing cards – quietly, as Mr Flyswotter had warned them. The rest were simply gazing into space, much to Mr Flyswotter's annoyance.

Two girls and two boys were doing crochet under Mrs Tallhat's supervision. They weren't making hats or anything else interesting however – just oven gloves.

Tony broke the gloomy silence by asking if he could read a story aloud.

Mr Flyswotter hesitated. "It would have to be a story we could learn something from," he insisted.

"Oh, it will be! You can learn a lot from my story," Tony promised him. "It's about the fight between good and evil."

"Really?" said Mr Flyswotter, obviously delighted. The other children made not-so-delighted faces. After what Tony had said, they were expecting him to read some sort of worthy and instructive text!

Tony went off gleefully to his room and came back with *The Vampire from Amsterdam* – the book Mrs Goody had given him from the Happy Valley community book collection. He opened it at one of his favourite stories: "James Bradley's Vampire" by Roger M. Thomas.

Without announcing the title, he began to read.

The longer Tony read, the more attentively the others listened.

The group gathered round Mrs Tallhat almost forgot to crochet. Only Mr Flyswotter's face grew longer and longer.

"And what, if you please, are we supposed to learn from this story?" he asked sarcastically, when Tony had finished.

"That even on a school trip, you can have an interesting evening!" giggled Viola, gazing at Tony. Tony looked away quickly.

Mr Flyswotter mumbled something no one could understand and, looking even more grumpy than before, ordered them all to their dormitories.

"And if anyone makes a noise, they'll have to stand out in the corridor all night!" he threatened.

Oh, no! thought Tony.

But this time Mr Flyswotter's words seemed to have the desired effect. Or perhaps everyone was just tired. In any case, shortly after ten o'clock, all was quiet.

Just as he had the night before, Tony climbed out of the window. Once outside, he noticed with a start that there was a light still burning in the building next door, where Mr Dredfel lived. Last night there had been no light. But yesterday he'd climbed out an hour later . . . What if the manager of the hostel decided to go on a final patrol round the house before he went to bed? The thought went scorching through Tony's mind.

Mr Flyswotter was no threat, because his room was on the other side of the hostel. Mrs Tallhat and Mrs Nutcake had two rooms up in the attic, Tony knew. He glanced up at the windows under the eaves. They were dark.

Suddenly, one of the windows opened, and he heard Viola's voice, "Tony?"

"Yes," he answered. "Where are you?"

She giggled. "In the girls' loo! Wait a minute, I'll be with you."

"The girls' loo – how nice!" said a rough voice suddenly, from behind Tony. He spun round and saw the Little Vampire.

"Oh, it's you, Rudolph," said Tony in surprise.

"Yeah," growled the Little Vampire. "And I'm fed up already."

"Fed up?"

"You said it! How would you like to hang about on the edge of the woods for hours and hours?"

Hours and hours? thought Tony to himself. Rudolph's exaggerations sometimes went quite over the top. It hadn't been dark all that long!

Out loud he said, "No, I wouldn't. But I could only come once everyone else was asleep. And anyway, you'd better go," he added.

"Go?" exploded the Little Vampire.

"Yes – till I've had a chance to tell Viola about you."

"What, haven't you told her about me yet?" exclaimed the Little Vampire indignantly. "That was the least I expected from a friend. You could have described all my good points to her!"

"Yes, well," said Tony, "I went for a different approach."

"A different approach? What's that supposed to mean?"

"Well, Viola doesn't know anything about you yet, does she?"

"Of course she doesn't know me," snorted the vampire, adding with a silly giggle, "It's such a pity that Viola and I haven't met yet!"

"Well, I don't think she'd have agreed to meet someone she didn't know at ten o'clock at night at the edge of the woods," Tony went on.

"No," the Little Vampire admitted.

"So I decided to arrange the meeting between Viola and *me*," said Tony.

"Hmmm . . ." The Little Vampire scratched his chin thoughtfully. "And then what? I mean, how will Viola and I end up together?"

"I'll talk her into coming on a moonlit walk with me, and then you can bump into us," explained Tony, "and I can introduce you. But now it really would be better if you went, Rudolph!" he urged.

"All right," said the Little Vampire. "But hurry up and persuade her!"

He moved away noiselessly. Tony watched till he had disappeared among the trees.

Ten on Each Finger

Suddenly, someone tapped Tony on the shoulder.

"Anna!" he cried.

He'd been meaning to ask her where she'd been hiding the whole time, but to his surprise, he found himself looking at – Viola!

"Anna?" Viola's mouth twitched. "You must have ten on each finger!"

"Ten what?" said Tony, mystified.

"Girlfriends! Ten girlfriends!" spat Viola.

"No, I've only got one," Tony told her – and at least that was true.

"What about this Anna, then?" asked Viola distrustfully.

"Anna? You must have misheard me," countered Tony. "When you tapped me on the shoulder, I thought it was Tanya, and so I said, 'Anya?' "

"Anya?"

"That's what I call her sometimes."

"It sounded like Anna," Viola persisted.

"Maybe." Tony cut off a grin. "But why would I have said Anna? There's no one in the class called Anna."

"That's true," Viola admitted. Then, after a pause, she asked in her usual direct fashion, "What happened about Tanya, anyway?"

"Tanya?"

"Yes! Haven't you finished with her after all?"

"Yes."

"So why did you think it was *her* tapping you on the shoulder?"

"You're right, I should have realized," said Tony quickly. "After all, you've got much softer hands than her!"

"Really?"

"And you move much more quietly."

Viola gave a smug grin. "Well, I didn't want to get caught by old Flyswotter."

That was the cue Tony was waiting for!

"Me neither," he said. "Why don't we walk on a bit? We could go into the woods. Then Mr Flyswotter will never hear us."

"But there are wolves and wild boars in the woods," answered Viola. Courage was obviously not her strong point.

"Wolves died out here years ago," Tony contradicted her. "And you only find wild boars deep in the forest, over by Devil's Rocks or even further away. In any case. I've got my torch."

Viola hesitated. "I don't know. . ."

At that moment, the light above the front door of Mr Dredfel's house came on. Almost at once, the door opened, and they heard someone clearing his throat.

"The manager! Quick! We'll have to hide!" whispered Tony. He grabbed Viola's arm and, pulling her with him, didn't stop running until they reached the edge of the woods.

"Ow!" said Viola, rubbing her arm.

"Sorry," said Tony, "but I had no idea Mr Dredfel was going to pop up!" To himself, he added, I do hope he doesn't discover there's a window open! Tony had pulled the window to, of course, but a puff of wind could easily blow it open again. . .

If the manager discovered the open window, he'd be bound to go and tell old Flyswotter. Then the two of them would probably search dormitories to find out who was missing. . .

How Nice!

'So what do we do now?" Tony heard Viola asking.

He pulled himself together. "What now?" he repeated.

"You kept going on about how 'romantic' it was in the woods didn't you?"

"Yeah."

"Huh! *I* can't see anything romantic about it. You can't even see the moon properly, let alone any shooting stars! And there are all those crackles and rustlings. I don't think it's at all romantic – I think it's spooky!"

"Spooky?" repeated Tony absent-mindedly. He was still thinking about Mr Dredfel and what would happen if he found out he wasn't in bed.

'Can't you at least switch on your torch?" hissed Viola.

"Yes, you could at least do that!" came a rough, throaty voice, and the Little Vampire slipped out from behind a bush. "It's not very polite of you to let this pretty young girl go on shivering with fright, and not do anything about it!"

Now Viola really was shaking. Rudolph's sudden appearance had even given Tony quite a scare.

Since he last saw him, the Little Vampire had obviously tried to make himself look a bit more "human", probably by using make-up – even in the dim light under the trees you could see his rouged cheeks. He had also sprinkled himself liberally with a very strong perfume, which smelled suspiciously like Anna's

Fragrance of Eternal Love.

Tony coughed.

"Yes, yes," nodded the Little Vampire. "You've got a lot to learn, when it comes to getting to know such an enchanting young lady as this one."

"Who's that?" asked Viola. She didn't look particularly frightened, anymore, just surprised.

"Where are your manners, Tony Peasbody?" snorted the Little Vampire to cover up his embarrassment. "Come on, introduce me to the young lady!"

Tony stretched out a hand. "This is Rudolph, a friend of mine," he explained, "and this is Viola, who has just joined our class."

"How nice!" murmured the Little Vampire, holding out a bony hand to Viola.

Viola took Rudolph's hand – and immediately dropped it again. She had obviously never touched such an icy hand before!

"Well, are you going to switch on your torch?" said the Little Vampire bossily. "I'm sure Viola would like to see more clearly who you've just introduced her to!"

"N-no!" Viola answered hastily.

"No?" repeated the Little Vampire, puzzled.

"Because of Mr Dredfel," breathed Viola. "He might see us."

"Oh, he went back inside his house ages ago," replied the Little Vampire.

"Really?" cried Tony. "Are you quite sure?"

"Of course!" snapped the Little Vampire. "Are you suggesting I would tell a lie?"

"No, of course not," said Tony quickly. "But he was out in the yard only ten minutes ago."

"Yes," The Little Vampire tapped his forehead. "And *five* minutes ago I heard him lock his door."

"Are you sure?" asked Tony, still not completely convinced.

"I certainly did!" thundered the Little Vampire.

Viola giggled. "You must have ears like a lynx!"

"Like a lynx?" Rudolph laughed dismissively. "We vampires have ears ten times better than a lynx!"

Tony's heart stopped beating in shock. What a stupid, careless thing to say! The Little Vampire didn't even seem to have noticed what he'd let slip! It was only when Viola asked tremulously, "Did you just say 'vampires'?" that Rudolph's eyes widened.

"V-vamp-p-pires?" he stammered. "I, um . . . " and he looked helplessly at Tony.

Tony set to work with determination. "Rudolph's an actor," he explained.

Viola pricked up her ears. "An actor?"

"Yes, in films," said Tony. "He's playing in a vampire film at the moment."

"Oh, so that's why he's wearing such an amazing outfit . . ." Viola's suspicions had obviously disappeared. "I was just thinking, such a fantastic costume could only be part of a film! And the mask is perfect, too!"

"What mask?" croaked the vampire.

"The mask you're using for the vampire film, of course!" Tony helped him. "You know!" he added imploringly.

But the Little Vampire seemed to be particularly slow at catching on this evening.

"No," he said, clicking his teeth. 'I *don't* know what you mean."

"Of course you do!" Tony insisted. "And you can rest assured, Rudolph, Viola's not an actress! She won't tell the reporters anything about your part in the film!"

"Reporters?" murmured the Little Vampire. He was obviously totally baffled.

"But I want to be an actress!" put in Viola, who hadn't been able to take her eyes off Rudolph ever since Tony had mentioned he was an actor.

I expect she's hoping for a part in his film! thought Tony, just managing to control a laugh.

"I suppose you've just finished the last take?" Viola began to question the Little Vampire.

But he only muttered, "Take? Taking what?"

Of course Tony knew what Viola was talking about. Each piece of filming starts with a clap of the famous black and white wooden clapperboards, and is called a "take": the last "take" was the last piece of filming for the day.

He grinned. In one sense, Viola had hit the nail on the head: Rudolph really was being "taken" for a ride – he didn't seem to have a clue what was going on!

"Perhaps we should change the subject," suggested Tony. "You see, Rudolph's so busy with filming that he'd rather not talk about it any more."

"What a shame!" It was clear from Viola's voice that she would have liked to pump Rudolph with questions for hours.

After a pause, she asked in a honey-sweet voice, "Perhaps you'd like to come and talk about it tomorrow, Rudolph?"

"Would you like us to meet up again tomorrow?" exclaimed the Little Vampire.

Viola nodded. "Oh yes, I really would!"

The Little Vampire could hardly believe his luck. "I . . . I'll be waiting for you," he muttered, his voice full of emotion.

"What about the shooting?" Viola wanted to know. "Will it go on so late tomorrow too?"

"Sh-shooting?" The vampire was lost.

"Yes, of course," Tony put in quickly. "Rudolph's scenes will be shot at the same time as today. After all, you *have* to shoot vampire films in the evening."

"Then I'll see you tomorrow, Rudolph," murmured Viola. "Bring me an autographed photo!"

She seemed to have forgotten about Tony. Ignoring him completely, she ran back to the youth hostel, giggling.

Really Nice

Once she was out of sight, the Little Vampire dug Tony in the ribs. "Now will you kindly explain what all that was about!" he demanded.

"Didn't you understand?" retorted Tony.

"Would I be asking you otherwise?" hissed the vampire.

"Well," said Tony, "I'll explain if you're nicer to me!"

"What!" roared the vampire. "I've been really nice to you all evening!"

"You have to Viola!" said Tony furiously. "But you just kept bellowing at me!"

"So?" The Little Vampire gave a broad grin. "There's only one person bellowing around here, and that's you!"

Tony was so angry that he'd raised his voice till it was quite loud – too loud, in fact. He looked nervously around him. Luckily, the windows in the hostel and in Mr Dredfel's house were still dark.

"At any rate, it's thanks to *me* that Viola wants to meet you again!" he said.

"You?"

"Yes! If I hadn't had that idea about a vampire film at the last moment . . ."

"What then?"

"Well, Viola would probably have gone running off to Mr Flyswotter and Mr Dredfel and told them that there was a vampire loose in the woods! But now she won't tell anyone about you – for her own sake."

"What do you mean, for her own sake?"

"I'm sure she's hoping that you'll get her a part in your vampire film!"

"Oh," said the Little Vampire. "I'm beginning to see . . ."

"You're quick!" said Tony with a grin.

"Do you really think Viola believes I'm an actor?" asked Rudolph after a pause.

"Didn't you hear her asking you for a signed photograph?" replied Tony.

"Yeah." The Little Vampire giggled proudly. "Actually, that didn't surprise me. After all, I've always known I'm rather good looking."

Tony bit his lips to stop himself laughing.

"But where am I going to get one?" Rudolph said. "After all, I can't be photographed."

"Just tell her you've run out of signed photos," suggested Tony. "Due to the huge demands of your fans."

"Run out?" grunted the Little Vampire. "No, I've got a better idea. I'll get my portrait drawn – in fact, *you* can do it!"

Tony gave a dry laugh. That was typical of Rudolph!

"I haven't got a pencil," he said.

"Then go and get one from the hostel!"

"I haven't got one there either," Tony told him.

"Well, how am I going to get a drawing with my signature on it then?" growled the Little Vampire.

"Why don't you ask Anna if she'll draw you?" said Tony.

Rudolph shook his head. "Anna can't. Her hand's swollen up like a pumpkin."

"Is she hurt?" asked Tony, shocked.

"Yes, a midge bit her." The vampire giggled.

"A midge?" repeated Tony. Rudolph was obviously having him on! At least three midges had bitten him on the hand since his arrival in Crumbletomb, but he was still able to write in his diary, worse luck!

"Is that why Anna hasn't come with you?" he asked.

The Little Vampire nodded. "She feels dizzy too. That's why she decided to stay in her coffin. Hmmm, perhaps Greg would draw me," he said, turning once more to his own problems, "*if* I ask him nicely! Oh, it'd be fantastic if Viola could take my picture around with her all the time . . ."

"It'd be completely bonkers if you ask me!" retorted Tony. "Just as bonkers as you blurting out just now that vampires have ten times better ears than a lynx!"

"I must fly!" hissed the Little Vampire, who didn't like being reminded of his own mistakes. "Can't you hear my tummy rumbling?"

"No," said Tony.

"Well, I can," insisted the vampire. Then he added, sounding unusually friendly, "Goodnight, Tony. And keep all your fingers crossed – for a good likeness!"

"Y-yes, of course I will," said Tony, puzzled at this sudden change of mood. The Little Vampire made a couple of powerful arm movements, and flew away.

Slowly, Tony walked back to the hostel. Everything was just as he had left it: the half-closed window, the empty, quiet passage. Even Olly was still snoring as he slipped silently back to bed.

His last thoughts before he fell asleep were of Anna. She must be quite badly hurt to want to stay behind in her coffin! But how could anyone get dizzy and have a hand blown up like a pumpkin, all from a midge bite? Tony just couldn't understand it. It must have been something else that had stung her. Or perhaps . . . she'd been bitten by something more dangerous than a midge.

Tony made up his mind to ask Mr Flyswotter next morning whether there might be any poisonous snakes in Crumbletomb after all.

Off to a Museum

But Tony never had the chance. Mr Flyswotter's threatened walk to the Barren Mountains was a washout, in the truest sense of the word, for by breakfast it was already raining hard. So Mr Flyswotter was forced to change his plans. After a discussion with Mrs Tallhat and Mrs Nutcake he announced they would drive to the nearby town and visit the museum there.

"Typical!" Olly complained on the way to the bus stop. "Off to a museum to look at stuffy old things! It's bad enough having to go there with a stuffy old teacher!"

"Perhaps they'll decide to keep Old Flyswotter as an exhibit!" Tony remarked with a grin.

"Yes, and then they'll put him in a glass case," joked Sebastian, "with a label round his neck: Teacher from one hundred years ago."

The museum was housed in what had once been a country mansion. Contrary to what the children had been expecting, it contained some really interesting items, like coaches.

Tony spent a long time looking at one of the coaches. He was fascinated by its huge black wheels, black wooden door and black leather awning. There was no label to tell him the history or the age of the coach, but it was obviously very old. Tony wondered with a slight shudder who might have travelled in it. The coach looked rather mysterious, as though it had been specially built for driving out at night. He was sure that Anna would be enchanted with it – and the other vampires too.

Viola must have had the same thought, for suddenly Tony heard her voice close by. "That'd be just right for Rudolph's film, don't you think?" she remarked.

"Y-yes."

"Do you think they've got a coach already?"

"I – I don't know," said Tony, looking round carefully. No way must Olly and the others find out that he was having a secret conversation here with Viola. Not because they'd all start gossiping about them – that didn't bother Tony at all. No, he was afraid that Viola's admirers would then start to spy on her day *and* night.

"We mustn't be seen together!" he said.

But Viola continued quizzing him: "What do you mean, you don't know whether they've got a coach? Rudolph must have told you whether it's a modern vampire film he's in, or an old-fashioned one with coaches and tumbledown graveyards." Rudolph's "shooting sequences" never seemed to be out of her thoughts.

"Of course it's not a *modern* film," said Tony. "But they – er – they've got a coach already. A much better one than this." Once more he glanced over at the door.

"Really? Does Rudolph drive about in this beautiful coach? I mean, in the film?"

"Yes." Tony was getting more and more nervous.

"Do you think I could see it sometime?"

"How?"

"I could visit Rudolph on the set!" Viola giggled. "Then I might get to go in the coach with him! Do you think he'd like that?"

Tony could hear footsteps coming nearer. He

answered quickly, "You'll have to ask Rudolph that this evening!"

Just then, up popped Henry and Olly.

Viola ran up to them. "Just take a look at this fantastic black coach!" she trilled. "It looks as if it's come straight from Count Dracula's castle in Transsiberia!"

Tony had to grin. Transylvania, more like! But he decided to keep the thought to himself.

"What's Tony got to do with it?" asked Henry, looking suspiciously from one to the other.

"Nothing at all," said Tony, strolling as casually as he could out of the room.

The Creeps

In the afternoon, when it had stopped raining, the walk that had been postponed from the morning took place. But luckily it was too late to go all the way to the Barren Mountains. Instead, Mr Flyswotter decided to steer a course towards a farmyard in the neighbourhood. It was supposed to be very special, a real little "picture-book" farm, as Mr Flyswotter told them enthusiastically, with lots of interesting animals. At the mention of "interesting animals", Tony suddenly remembered Anna's swollen hand.

"You know we were talking about snakes," he began, walking along beside Mr Flyswotter. "Do you think there might be poisonous snakes in Crumbletomb after all?"

Mr Flyswotter's face took on a vexed expression. "You and your poisonous snakes!" he scolded. "Why does there always have to be something sensational! You get your kicks from creeps and horrors – it all comes from too much television!"

"But there *could* be poisonous snakes, couldn't there?" Tony persisted.

"Well, yes," Mr Flyswotter admitted reluctantly. "In places that have lain undisturbed for a long time. You know of course that snakes are frightened of humans – and not the other way round."

"These places where you might find poisonous snakes . . . Could you find rare herbs and plants there too?"

asked Tony boldly.

"You might indeed," Mr Flyswotter told him. "Or did you think rare plants grew along the roadside?"

Normally, Tony would have been irritated by Mr Flyswotter's headmasterly tone, but just now he was much too agitated. If it was true that rare plants grew in places where there were still poisonous snakes about, then he was right to be concerned about Anna's injury!

"What sort of poisonous snakes would they be?" inquired Tony, ignoring the fact that Mr Flyswotter was looking more and more annoyed.

"Adders," replied Mr Flyswotter, who taught Tony's class biology as well as maths. "Tell me, didn't you get a B for biology?"

Tony nodded. He had, but at this rate, he would probably never get a B again! The things he did for Anna! But he had to ask one last question: "If you get bitten by an adder, is it very dangerous?" He could hear his voice quiver as he spoke.

"Yes, indeed it is," Mr Flyswotter told him. "There's only one thing to do: suck the poison out, bandage the arm or leg firmly, and get the patient to the nearest doctor as quickly as possible."

The thought shot through Tony's mind: "Poor Anna!" Not, of course, that she would die . . . But she'd have to stay in her coffin with a temperature and shivers, and horrible pain.

"Is *that* the farm?" Olly interrupted his thoughts. In front of them lay a building with white plastic window frames, a crude aluminium door, fibreglass tiles and a red corrugated iron roof. It didn't look in the least like a "picture-book farm" – more like some hideous house from the suburbs.

"They must have had it renovated," said Mr

Flyswotter. "When I was here last time, the house had a thatched roof and leaded windows and the door had the most attractive and artistic carvings."

"Now they've got a motorbike instead," Sebastian remarked.

"It's terrible what's happened to this beautiful old farmyard!" Mr Flyswotter couldn't contain himself.

"I don't expect there are any interesting animals left either," said Olly. And he was right.

The farmer, who even remembered Mr Flyswotter – although five years had gone by since his last school trip to Crumbletomb – had changed his operation to fattening pigs and dairy cattle "because of subsidies from the government", as he told them proudly.

On the way home, Mr Flyswotter looked extremely depressed.

"Well," said Tony to Olly, "it certainly gave you the creeps, but not in the usual way!"

"Do you want us to write about the 'picture-book' farm?" asked Henry, when they were sitting once again in the hostel with their diaries open in front of them.

"No, no," grunted Mr Flyswotter hastily. "Just write about the museum." Then, in his usual strict teacher's voice, he added, "I think you should have enough material there!"

Any Amount of Good Words

After tea, Mr Flyswotter organized another, longer walk. "Otherwise you won't be able to get to sleep!" he explained.

Tony had been worrying about that, because no one had done anything particularly exhausting that day. What would happen to the meeting between Rudolph and Viola if the others stayed awake till midnight or even later? Tony hadn't actually fixed a time with the Little Vampire, but only because they'd agreed to meet up as early as possible – around ten o'clock, as they had the evening before.

That was why Tony suggested they should play a couple more games and races, after which they were all quite exhausted. It helped: by a quarter to ten, all his room mates were fast asleep.

Quietly, Tony got out of bed.

There was no one in the passage. The door to Mr Flyswotter's room stood half open, and Tony could hear monotonous organ music coming from inside. Mr Flyswotter had probably nodded off in front of his portable radio!

Even so, Tony was careful to avoid making a noise. He tiptoed down to the dining room and let himself out of the window in the usual way.

Once outside, he took a deep breath. It struck him that each evening it was getting a bit harder to leave the

hostel. He looked over towards Mr Dredfel's house. There was only one small window on the first floor with a light. Could the manager be in bed already?

He went on, cautiously – and nearly let out a cry. A figure suddenly detached itself from the shadow of a tree and came over to him – a vampire Tony realized, his mind in a whirl. But a vampire Tony had never seen before, with fair hair standing up round its head like a crown, and eyes deepset in shadowy sockets . . .

It was only when the vampire asked with a giggle, "Did I give you a fright?" that he realized it was Viola!

"Wh-where did you get all that gear?" he stammered. Viola's costume looked almost perfect: she had whitened her skin with make-up, drawn dark rings round her eyes, and outlined her lips in red. Her hair was brushed into an untidy vampire frizz and she was wearing black tights and black ballet shoes. Her black pullover, worn instead of a vampire cloak, was the only thing out of place.

She giggled again. "Do you think I look convincing?"

"Convincing?" Tony hesitated.

"Yes, for the vampire film," she said excitedly. "Do you know, I'd like to act something out in front of Rudolph. If he likes it, perhaps he'll be able to get me a part in the film!"

"Oh, I see . . ."

She tugged at her pullover. "This outfit obviously isn't as good as Rudolph's. But it'll do for a first impression, anyway."

"A first impression?"

"Yes – of how I'd be as a vampire!"

"You look great!"

"Really?" she said, sounding pleased. "Do you think Rudolph will think so too?"

"I'm sure he will!" Tony assured her.

"Then perhaps he'll put in a good word for me," she lisped.

"Rudolph would put in any amount of good words for you," Tony declared. "The question is, whether it'll do any good."

"Are you saying the film people don't listen to him?" asked Viola anxiously. Then, suddenly suspicious, she asked, "Has Rudolph only got a minor role in the vampire film?"

"Oh, no!" Tony told her. "He's got the main part. Do you think he'd have such a splendid costume if he only had a minor role?"

"The main part . . ." said Viola thoughtfully. "I thought so. *I* would have given Rudolph the main part, if I'd been the director!" She sighed. "When do you think he'll come?"

"He ought to be here by now," said Tony, who had already been glancing around surreptitiously. Perhaps Rudolph was late because of Anna? Tony suddenly felt faint at the thought.

"Let's go," he said.

"Is Mr Dredfel out and about again?" asked Viola, peering across at the manager's house, which had gone completely dark during the time they had been talking.

"No, he's already asleep," Tony reassured her. "Rudolph likes meeting us in the forest because it's more romantic," he added.

"Oh, that's so like Rudolph – to be all romantic!"

"Yes, he's got a certain tendency towards it."

"That's what makes good acting!" declared Viola. "An actor has to have strong feelings about things!"

"Really?"

"Yes! For instance, Rudolph would never be able to play a vampire if he couldn't *feel* like one."

"Is that so?" said Tony in surprise. "Do you think he always feels like a vampire? I mean, once filming has finished?"

"That's how it is for lots of actors," Viola told him, rather grandly. "They can't tell the difference between their real personality and the part they're playing."

Tony and Viola had reached the edge of the woods by then, and there stood the Little Vampire, waiting for them, a broad grin on his face. Tony had already noticed him, but Viola had not. "Actors sometimes don't know who they really are eventually," she babbled on cheerfully.

"But *I* know who I am!" retorted the Little Vampire, with his grating laugh. "I am Rudolph Sackville-Bagg, the greatest actor of all time!"

"Rudolph, you . . ." murmured Viola.

"Hallo, Viola!" said Rudolph huskily.

Oddly enough, it didn't bother Tony that the Little Vampire was ignoring him. For one thing, he hadn't expected anything different – he knew that Rudolph was trying to look as grown-up as possible in front of Viola. For another thing, Tony thought it was much more important that at last he seemed to be getting over his mental depression.

"You're looking really great!" the Little Vampire was saying to Viola. "You should always wear black!"

She laughed affectedly. "Do you think so?"

"Yes! From a distance, I almost thought you were —" Rudolph broke off.

Tony guessed he had been about to say "a real vampire", but had stopped himself at the last moment.

"An actress?" asked Viola hopefully.

"Exactly!" cried the vampire. "An actress from my vampire film, ha, ha!"

He threw Tony a look of triumph. He was probably waiting for his friend to applaud.

"I just need a cloak," Viola complained, tugging unhappily at her pullover. "But I'm sure you've got more vampire cloaks in the properties box, haven't you?"

"In the – what?" asked Rudolph.

"Well, in the place where you keep all the costumes!"

"Oh, I see!" The Little Vampire tapped his forehead. "*That's* where you meant. Yes, yes, we've got heaps of vampire cloaks!" he boasted.

"Oh, then I'm sure you can bring me one!" giggled Viola.

The Little Vampire hesitated. "Bring you one?"

"Yes, then you'll like me even more!" she giggled.

"Hmm, well . . ." Rudolph looked helplessly at Tony.

"I'm not sure Rudolph's producer would go along with that," said Tony.

"Why not?" asked Viola. "If they've got heaps and heaps of vampire cloaks!"

"Well, you see . . ." Tony cleared his throat. "The cloaks are very valuable, they're made of special cloth, and so —"

"That's right!" the Little Vampire agreed. "But I'll have a word with the pro – producer. If he knew it was for a friend of *mine* . . ."

Showered with Prizes

"Now I want to give you your present!" announced the Little Vampire, changing the subject quickly.

He groped under his cloak and, with a bow, presented Viola with something that looked like a piece of paper.

"Thank you, Rudolph," breathed Viola.

"Don't you know what it is?" asked the Little Vampire, as she stood turning the paper over and over, looking puzzled.

"To tell you the truth, no," she answered.

"It must be the signed photograph!" suggested Tony.

"Hey! Don't put your nose in here!" snapped the Little Vampire.

"*Is* it your picture?" asked Viola excitedly.

The Little Vampire giggled conceitedly, before admitting, "Yes!"

"How kind of you, Rudolph! To think that you remembered!" Viola turned the card over once more, but it was much too dark to see anything – at least, for human eyes. "Are all your films listed on the back?"

"My films?"

"Yes – all the parts you've played and all the awards you've been given . . ."

"Awards?" repeated the Little Vampire stupidly.

"You *have* been given awards, haven't you?" asked Viola.

"Me?" The Little Vampire looked completely at a loss.

But how could he know about the customs of modern culture?

"Of course he's been given some!" Tony sprang to his defence. "More than you could possibly list on a tiny autographed picture!"

As he said this, he looked anxiously at the Little Vampire. He just hoped Rudolph wouldn't let on how totally clueless he was about films! But the Little Vampire simply clicked his teeth and kept quiet.

"I bet Rudolph's latest film will be showered with prizes for its costumes alone!" said Viola. "Yes, and then there are the other actors. Who else is playing with you?" she asked curiously, after a pause.

Tony caught a puzzled look from the Little Vampire. Rudolph, of course, didn't know the name of a single living actor!

"Who's playing?" repeated Tony. "That's a closely guarded secret!"

"Yes, it's a secret!" repeated the Little Vampire, sounding relieved.

"What a pity!" said Viola. Then, sounding disappointed, she asked, "I suppose the filming's all taking place in secret too?"

"Yes, absolutely!" said Tony vigorously.

Viola turned to Rudolph. "Won't they make any exceptions?" she asked, in a voice of melting sweetness.

"Ex-exceptions?" stammered the Little Vampire. "T-to what?" He had obviously only been listening to her flattering tone, and not at all to what she had actually been saying!

"Well, to their decision to keep it all secret." Viola gave a charming giggle. "I would *so* like to see you playing your part, Rudolph!"

"Really?"

"Yes! Don't you think your producer might make a teeny-weeny exception just this once – for us?"

"For us . . ." sighed the Little Vampire.

"There's no way he would!" Tony said firmly, interrupting all this billing and cooing.

"Haven't I just told you to keep out of this?" The Little Vampire turned on him angrily.

"You did say so," agreed Tony, "but I don't think you meant it. Or do you really want to show Viola the "film set"?"

"Yes!" spat the vampire, only to change his mind immediately. "N-no."

"The film's nearly finished," said Tony to Viola, trying to pacify her. "But of course you'll be the most important guest at the world première – you'll even get to sit next to Rudolph!"

"I'll be the most important guest?" Viola gave a squeal of excitement. "And I'll sit next to Rudolph?"

"Yes, in the front row," Tony promised her.

A Dramatic Exit

"Be quiet!" the Little Vampire suddenly cried. "Will you two be quiet!"

Turning away with a sob, he vanished among the trees before Tony could recover from his surprise.

"Do you think that was a scene from his film?" asked Viola.

"From his film?" repeated Tony.

"Well, it was certainly a dramatic exit!" Viola giggled. "After all, most people at least say goodbye," she babbled. "But then I suppose actors are like that . . ."

She gave a happy sigh. "Do you think Rudolph had to go back to work?"

"Work? No," murmured Tony.

He'd just remembered that he'd never asked how Anna was.

"Perhaps they decided to go on filming into the ghostly hours," Viola gave an affected laugh. "That's what often happens when they make a film," she went on, as though she was an expert. "So that they can – how do they put it? – 'capture the atmosphere'. Yes, that's it – capture the atmosphere!"

"No, they certainly won't be doing any more filming today," Tony contradicted her. "Rudolph simply wanted to rest before tomorrow's shooting. We ought to be getting back too."

"Yes, let's go," said Viola. "I want to have a good look

at the details on the back of Rudolph's signed photo: when and where he was born, how he was 'discovered', what his first part was and, of course, what awards he's won . . ."

Tony grinned to himself but said nothing. He was quite sure that none of these facts would be found on Rudolph's "signed photograph"!

They had reached the hostel. To his relief, he found that all was still dark.

"How do you get back inside?" whispered Viola.

Tony pointed to the dining room. "Through that little window. It's only pushed to."

Viola took a key from under her pullover. "I go through the laundry room! Why don't you come too?" she asked. "It's much more comfortable!"

Tony shook his head. "No. It'd be bad enough if one of us were caught. But both of us together – that would be a catastrophe!"

"Yes, you're right," Viola giggled. "Goodnight!"

She darted away and Tony watched her go. She was probably already imagining how all eyes would be drawn to her on the day of the world première, and how the director would offer her a part in his new film!

He almost burst out laughing at the thought, even though he wasn't feeling at all cheerful. He thought anxiously of Anna, and he was also worried about the Little Vampire. He could still hear Rudolph's "Be quiet! Will you two be quiet!" and the vampire's loud sobs as he vanished among the trees.

Tony thought he knew what had made the vampire cry: their conversation about the film that would never be shot, about the world première that would always be a dream, and about Viola, who would never sit next to him in the front row as the most important guest . . . All these things had made Rudolph realize, in the most painful way, that as a vampire he was forever excluded from a normal life.

All this just at a time when Rudolph was already depressed about the failure of Mr Crustscrubber's course of treatment, and Olga's sudden departure with Aunt Dorothy . . . He was sure the Little Vampire had flown straight back to the vault, to creep back into his coffin feeling sorry for himself. And there in the vault would be Anna, with her injured hand . . .

Tony suddenly made up his mind: he would fetch his vampire cloak, pick up his torch and fly back to the cemetery himself!

Talking about Biting...

The church clock stood at half past eleven when Tony reached the cemetery and flew along the wall in the shadow of the tall trees. The Sackville-Bagg family vault lay at the far end, in the old, unkempt part of the graveyard. Not long before, McRookery the Nightwatchman, and his assistant Sniveller, had tried to turn it into a "garden" – with the secret aim of getting rid of the vampires at the same time.

McRookery and Sniveller had indeed succeeded in chasing the Sackville-Bagg family out of their vault with their diggers and bulldozers and the vampires had been forced to move to the ruins in the Vale of Doom.

But then, under the leadership of Mr Crustscrubber, a petition from the townspeople to "Save the Old Cemetery" had managed to stop the destruction of the graveyard, and so the vampires had come back again.

Now, in the moonlight, Tony could see that the grass was growing tall and thick once more. And there was the old yew tree, under which lay the entrance to the vault.

He felt his throat tighten at the thought of the narrow shaft down which he would have to slide in order to reach Anna and Rudolph.

He landed behind a bush and, with a thumping heart, looked over at the yew tree.

Whatever else happened, he would have to find out whether the Little Vampire and Anna were alone in the vault before he pushed aside the stone covering the entrance hole. But how could he do that without putting himself in danger? Tony looked around uneasily. He now thought his decision to fly back here had been altogether too hasty and thoughtless. But it was too late!

He decided to wait a little longer. Perhaps Anna or Rudolph would come out of the vault . . . He made himself as small as he could behind the bush. It wasn't the first time he'd been alone at night in the cemetery, but he would never get used to the fear that always seemed to creep over him! The noises alone were bad enough: all those creakings and cracklings, and the rustling and hissing in the treetops. . .

The night was alive – a thousand times more alive than you could possibly imagine when you were at home, tucked up in your warm, cosy bed! And the night had thousands of eyes – eyes that remained invisible to Tony. But they were watching him, because they could see in the dark. . .

Tony felt his hair beginning to stand on end. He looked over once more at the entrance hole, and, as though his words could conjure them up, he spoke aloud, urgently but softly, "Rudolph, Anna, I'm here!"

"And *I* am here!" All of a sudden he heard a husky voice behind him.

Tony spun round as if electrified – and found himself staring into the pale face of Greg.

"Well, well, what a surprise!" said Greg in mock friendliness. "Tony Peasbody, come to visit us in our nice old graveyard!"

Then, in quite a different voice, he thundered, "What are you looking for here?"

"I — " Tony gulped. "I wanted to see Rudolph – and Anna. She's not well, is she?"

"Not well?" Greg clicked his long, pointed teeth together. "You could say that Anna's learning her lesson the hard way."

"Learning her lesson?"

"Yes. Paying for it. Get it?"

"No," Tony admitted.

"If she goes on like this, she'll never pass the test!" Greg went on maliciously.

An icy shudder ran through Tony. "H-her test?" he stuttered. "To be – a vampire?"

Greg tapped his forehead. "Good grief!" he groaned. "You really are slow, aren't you? Anna's already a hopeless case as far as being a vampire is concerned."

"And anyway," he added in a menacing undertone, "that's mostly your fault, Tony Peasbody!"

"My fault?" echoed Tony.

Greg nodded meaningfully. "You've said it! As far as I can gather, *you* don't want to be a vampire . . ." Then, with a scornful laugh, he added, "and that's something *I* find totally incomprehensible, ha, ha!"

Tony thought it wiser to say nothing. "This test," he asked cautiously, "what subject is Anna taking?"

"The science of herbs of course, stupid!" replied Greg.

"Science of herbs?"

"Yes. What plants are good for tummyache, headache, toothache . . . Plants for making perfume and smelling salts . . . In other words, everything a vampire might need! Or did you think we can simply go to a chemist's shop and buy things like that?"

" 'Course I didn't!" said Tony.

"Now you see", went on Greg, more gently, "why we always have an expert on herbs."

"And that's Anna?"

"Wrong again! It's our grandmother, Sabina the

Sinister. But Anna volunteered to take over the job. Our dear grandmother is getting more and more forgetful, and that can have unpleasant consequences."

"Like it did for Anna!" Tony couldn't help himself saying.

"What do you mean?"

"Well, she got bitten by a snake, while she was out collecting herbs, didn't she?"

"Who's been telling you stories?" Greg asked in amusement.

"No one," said Tony hastily. 'I thought it out for myself."

"You'd better leave thinking to those who have bigger brains than you!" giggled Greg.

"Do you mean Anna hasn't been bitten by a snake?"

Tony felt his heart grow lighter, in spite of having Greg right there next to him.

"No, she has *not* been bitten by a snake," Greg told him gruffly. Then, he added, with a malicious grin, "But since we're talking about biting, Tony Peasbody, I've suddenly had an idea. . .'

He opened his mouth wide, and Tony could see his hideous vampire teeth gleaming in the moonlight.

He shuddered. He mustn't show how frightened he was – he ought to distract Greg, get him to think about something else!

"But Anna's hand *is* injured," he said. "Rudolph told me."

"Rudolph, Rudolph!" echoed Greg dully. "Why are you always going on about Rudolph?"

Already he was raising his broad, powerful hands. . .

"Do you think Anna would be pleased to see me?" asked Tony quickly, taking a step backwards. His right foot struck an overturned gravestone, and he almost fell.

"Anyone round here would be pleased to see you!" answered Greg.

Tony pulled himself together.

"Is Anna alone in the vault? I mean, alone with Rudolph?"

"Rudolph?" thundered Greg, drawing himself up to his full height. "Do you know, you're really getting up my nose with your endless 'Rudolph, Rudolph'!"

"Am I?" Tony pretended to feel guilty.

"Completely and utterly!" spat Greg.

Then, to Tony's surprise, he asked, "Why don't you ever think of visiting *me* for a change?"

"Y-you?" stammered Tony.

"Yes! I'm sure we wouldn't get bored with each other!" Greg wrung his enormous hands and gave a husky laugh.

Better Safe than Sorry!

"To start with, we could do something fun . . ." said Greg after a pause.

Tony was scared. It sounded as though the vampire was making plans, and he didn't have the slightest desire to go off and do anything with the unpredictable and aggressive Greg!

"We could fly off to the park and have a race round the paddling pool," Greg suggested. "Or we could go to the cinema. There might be a horror film on!"

"I don't feel like going to the cinema today," Tony told him hurriedly. I've already had enough horrors, thank you, he added to himself.

"All right then, we'll go and give somebody a fright!" When there was no reaction from Tony, he hissed, "Hey, what's the matter? Have you got any ideas of your own?"

"I don't know —"

"What don't you know?" growled Greg, looking menacingly at Tony.

"Whether I wouldn't rather go and visit Anna," explained Tony. "Before!" he added hastily, so as not to provoke Greg.

"Before?" repeated Greg suspiciously.

"Yes, before we go off somewhere." Tony told himself he'd try to dissuade Greg from the idea of going off together, once he was in the vault.

"What do you mean?" Greg was beside himself with rage. "I, Gruesome Gregory, am going to have to wait till Tony Peasbody's finished handy-holding with my little sister?"

"No!" Tony contradicted him. "I just want to have a quick word with her."

Greg's mouth twisted. "A quick word? All right then. But no more than five minutes. And I'll be watching the church clock!"

"Aren't you going to come down to the vault with me?" asked Tony. He felt a cold shudder as he thought of the dark, narrow shaft.

Greg shook his head. "There's no clock in the vault. I'll wait for you up here."

"Couldn't you come with me?" pleaded Tony. "I mean, because of your family?"

"What have they got to do with it?"

"You could go on ahead and see whether any of them are still in the vault!"

"Go on ahead and look?" Greg pointed a finger at Tony and grinned. "Are you . . . frightened?"

"N-no!" said Tony. "I'm just being careful."

"Better safe than sorry!" grinned Greg. "Anyway, I can assure you that all my relatives are out. They're at a meeting of vampire elders."

"All of them? Even your parents?"

"Of course. What did you think? They're over a hundred and seventy years old, so they've been vampire elders for ages."

Tony cleared his throat. "What if one of them comes back unexpectedly?"

"From the meeting of elders? Never!" Greg reassured him. "They'll be celebrating till cockcrow!"

Tony looked uneasily over towards the yew tree.

"You said five minutes . . . " he began. "Couldn't we agree on *ten* minutes?"

"What, as long as that?" growled Greg. "Didn't you say just a quick word?"

"Yes, of course. But I've got to get down there first . . ."

"All right," agreed Greg generously. "Nine minutes. But not a second longer!"

Tony nodded. Nine minutes would have to do! Slowly, and with beating heart, he crept across to the yew tree.

"Hey, why are you slinking about like that?" Greg called after him. "Better hurry up, or there'll be trouble!"

"Y-yes," murmured Tony. His legs seemed to be getting heavier with every step.

At last he reached the entrance hole. With shaking hands, he pushed the flat, moss-covered stone to one side. The smell of decay and cool, damp earth rushed up at him, mixed with a familiar perfume: it was "Fragrance of Eternal Love".

"Anna!" he murmured, and suddenly he wasn't afraid any more. Anna had made the perfume out of the roses growing in the cemetery, just for the two of them. Perhaps it really did have magic powers!

He glanced over at Greg once more.

"Hurry up!" Greg hissed.

So Tony slid, legs first, down into the shaft.

Your Best Friend

As Tony landed on the firmly packed earth at the bottom, he heard Anna's voice. "Greg?" She sounded far away and strangely weak.

"It's me!" he answered.

"You, Tony?" the voice seemed to brighten.

"Yes!" Tony pushed the stone back over the entrance hole. "Are you alone?" he called into the vault, where a faint candlelight glimmered.

"No!" came the answer.

"No?" Tony's heart beat faster. "Is Rudolph with you?"

Anna giggled. "No!"

"Who then?" Tony asked nervously.

"My best friend," replied Anna.

For a moment, Tony was mystified. "Your best friend?"

"Yes – you!" Anna giggled again.

"Oh, I see," murmured Tony. Blushing, he came down the steps into the vault.

He saw with relief that the coffins were closed – all except the smallest. Anna was sitting in it, looking over at him with the sweetest smile – a smile which gave Tony the strangest feeling inside.

"I – I just came to see how you were," he said quickly.

"Did you?" Anna lifted her right hand, which was bandaged with a piece of old cloth. "My fingers are very swollen and feel as if they're burning."

"What happened to your hand?" asked Tony

anxiously, coming nearer. A single slim candle burned in an alcove in the wall, and by its feeble light, he thought Anna looked really ill and frail.

"It's an allergy," Anna explained. "I'm allergic to one of the plants, according to my grandmother, Sabina the Sinister." She pointed to a black, well-thumbed book which lay in her lap. "I'm trying to find out what sort of plant it was."

"Is that why you want to be an expert on herbs?" asked Tony.

"Me? An expert on herbs? Who told you that?"

"Greg!"

"Oh, it's so easy to pull the wool over *his* eyes! I made up all that business about gathering plants so that I'd be allowed to visit you at the hostel! Although," she added, looking at her bandaged hand, "at the moment I wish I *did* know a bit more about the healing power of plants!"

"Does it hurt a lot?"

"Quite a bit. And it makes me feel dizzy when I get up. All because of you!" Anna smiled.

"Me?"

"Yes, because I wanted to visit you so much. And because of Rudolph too, of course – I had to do something to get him out of his mental depression!"

Anna fiddled with a strand of her long, tangled hair. "I'm so pleased he's out and about with humans again," she said. "I bet he and Viola are crooning at each other right now."

"No, they're not," Tony told her sadly.

"What?" Anna was taken aback. "What are they doing then?"

"Nothing," he said in embarrassment. "Rudolph ran off when we started talking about his world première."

"What world première?"

"Viola thinks Rudolph's an actor – a film star."

Anna put her left hand – the one that wasn't hurt – to her mouth and gave a gurgling laugh. "Rudolph – a film star?"

Tony nodded. "This evening he even gave Viola a signed picture of himself."

"A signed picture? Where did he get that?"

"I think it was just a drawing Greg did of him."

"Then he ran away?" asked Anna after a pause.

"Yes."

"He'll turn up again," she said, not in the least concerned.

"I thought he'd be back here in the vault," said Tony. Then, with a sudden flash of inspiration, he added, "Actually, I wanted to invite him to our farewell party the day after tomorrow."

"Farewell party?" Anna looked at him with enormous eyes.

Tony cleared his throat. He didn't know exactly how he'd come to make this invitation – especially since it wasn't at all certain that the party would ever take place. But he couldn't take it back now. After all, Mr Flyswotter had more or less agreed to a party.

"We're having a party because it's our last evening," Tony told her boldly. "With a disco and all that."

Anna said nothing.

"You're invited too, of course," Tony remembered to say just in time. Anna's eyes were already glistening as though she were about to cry.

That's all I need! thought Tony, adding quickly, "You wouldn't let your best friend down, would you?"

"No," whispered Anna in a trembling voice. "But I don't know if I'll be able to fly by then."

"I'm sure you will!" said Tony.

At the thought of "flying", he suddenly remembered that Greg was waiting for him at the entrance to the vault . . . And not only that, he was sure he'd gone over the nine minutes that Greg had allowed him!

Really Peeved

"You've got to help me!" he begged Anna. "Greg's waiting outside for me!"

"Greg?" said Anna in surprise.

"He wants to go on an outing with me," Tony told her. "Frightening people, things like that. But *I* don't feel in the least bit like going!"

"Have you fixed a time to meet?"

"Yes, worse luck! Now I'm wondering how I can get him to change his mind."

"Change his mind?" Anna looked doubtful. "Greg always gets really peeved if you break an appointment with him!"

"Peeved?"

"Well, you know what he's like! No one gets angry as quickly as him!"

Tony felt his legs go weak. "You mean, I *have* to go on this outing?"

"There's only one way out, if you don't want to go flying with him," Anna replied.

"What's that?"

"The emergency exit! Greg doesn't just get angry quickly – he forgets quickly, too. If he doesn't manage to catch you today, he'll have forgotten the whole thing in a week at the most."

"Do you think so?" murmured Tony.

Shuddering, he looked over at the other coffins. He

recognized the big black one with the letter "T" carved on it surrounded by two snakes' heads, which had belonged to Theodore. This coffin had stood empty ever since McRookery the Nightwatchman had spied Uncle Theodore playing cards and had crept up and destroyed him with a wooden stake. . .

"This emergency exit," said Tony uneasily, "does it still go through Uncle Theodore's coffin?"

"Yes, although as you know, we've now got two emergency exits," Anna reminded him proudly. "The new one starts over there, in the corner."

She pointed to a gravestone leaning against the wall, which Tony hadn't noticed before.

"You'll be able to walk through our new emergency exit without stooping," Anna told him. "It comes out at the compost heap. Then you have to push the big tree stump over to one side."

"Tony shrugged his shoulders doubtfully. "I don't think I'll manage that on my own."

"I can't help you this time," said Anna regretfully.

"Well, there's nothing for it but the old one," muttered Tony. He would much rather have used the new emergency exit, because the old one ended in the well, not very far from the bushes where Greg was lurking.

But if he moved very, very gently and quietly . . . Greg wouldn't be watching the well; he'd be concentrating on the yew tree and the entrance to the vault!

"I'll be off then," said Tony. "See you the day after tomorrow – at the hostel!"

Anna smiled sweetly. "I'll do everything I can to be there. And then we'll dance together, promise?"

"Yes." Tony felt rather uncomfortable at the thought

of Rudolph and Anna with Mr Flyswotter close by. But he quickly pushed the thought away. At the moment, he had more urgent problems to think about!

He went over to Uncle Theodore's coffin and tugged at the two golden handles. It gave a jerk. He redoubled his efforts, and the lid slid to one side.

Tony shone his torch inside the coffin. The floor was covered with a layer of dust a centimetre thick, as if the old emergency exit hadn't been used for weeks and weeks. At the head end of the coffin he could see an opening cut out of the wood, leading down under the ground. It was just big enough for one person – or vampire, rather – to squeeze through.

He felt his heart beat fast.

He looked over at Anna. She was so small and fragile.

" 'Bye, Anna – get well soon!" he said.

"Good luck, Tony!" she wished him.

"Thanks," he said. He would certainly need luck – especially with Greg!

Hesitantly, Tony climbed into Uncle Theodore's coffin. He knelt down and pulled the lid back over the top. Then, coughing violently because of the clouds of dust, he crept down into the emergency exit.

There was Something!

Tony let the beam of light from his torch glide over the walls. With a shudder, he remembered his first and only "visit" down here. He had only had a spindly candle then, and it had flickered all the time. In the end it had gone out, and he'd been left in total darkness! Ugh! He shivered.

But his torch wouldn't let him down – he'd taken care of that already. Just that afternoon he'd put new batteries in it.

He crept further along. After a few metres, he saw a heart scratched on the wall with the initials "A + T" inside – he guessed they stood for Anna and Tony. After the question mark that Tony had scrawled next to the heart last time, there were now two fat exclamation marks. He had to smile, in spite of the grim surroundings. The emergency passage was coming to an end. Tony recognized the slab of marble closing the exit.

As soon as he reached the stone, he switched off his torch, just in case the beam of light could be seen from the cemetery above! Tony knew from past experience that the marble slab didn't completely shut off the opening.

He waited until his eyes had grown used to the darkness, then he began to push the heavy stone aside. It was hard work, but he managed in the end.

While he was getting his breath, he caught the sound

of footsteps on the gravel, and then voices.

"It was over there!" came a man's voice.

Tony's hair stood on end. It was the voice of McRookery, the Nightwatchman!

"I didn't see anything," answered a second, rather nasal voice, belonging unmistakably to Sniveller, the Assistant Gardener.

"But there *was* something! Over by the well!" retorted McRookery. The footsteps came nearer, and suddenly a strong beam of light was directed at the well. Tony had such a shock he almost cried out loud.

But then the light went out and McRookery grumbled crossly, "Nothing there!"

"And you got me out of bed just for this?" Sniveller complained. "If you only knew what a lovely dream I was having – a holiday on the Isle of Wight, and you quite well again."

"Fiddlesticks!" said McRookery gruffly. "I *am* quite well again, thank you! You can see that by the way my fingers are itching to put an end to those vampires, that band of bloodsuckers!"

His fingers itched . . . Tony thought of the sharpened wooden stakes that McRookery always carried around with him. Brrr! He made himself even smaller.

"But the doctor said you must take care of yourself for a while," Sniveller warned him.

"That doctor!" McRookery gave a scornful laugh. "He's got no idea what slack ways and lazy habits people have got into here while I've been away!"

"Slack ways? Lazy habits?" said Sniveller indignantly. "Nothing like that has happened while *I've* been in charge! I did what I could!"

"And that wasn't a lot!" remarked McRookery.

"Now you're being unfair," whined Sniveller. "I filled

in for you as best I could while you were in hospital!"

"Oh yes?" growled McRookery. "You've been twiddling your thumbs and taking it easy!"

"I have not!"

"You have!" said McRookery. "Have you caught a single vampire in all the weeks when – darn it! – I wasn't able to see that everything was in order?"

"No," Sniveller admitted in a small voice.

"Well then! Instead you made sure you lazed the days away, and then at night – when a Nightwatchman's work properly starts – you simply bolted the door!"

"I . . . I didn't want to spoil anything for you as far as vampire hunting goes," stammered Sniveller.

You Down There, Me Up Here!

"But now we're back together again," Sniveller went on eagerly. "Now we can join forces and wage war on them!" And in a loud voice, put on to impress McRookery, he cried out, "Down with the tribe of vampires! Down with the pack of bloodsuckers!"

"Ssssh!" hissed McRookery. "Have you taken leave of the last bit of sense you had?"

"What do you mean?" said Sniveller, puzzled.

"You shouldn't be making any noise," answered McRookery. "I've told you a thousand times: treading quietly is the first duty of a Nightwatchman! There, now you'll have to climb down into that old well!"

"Me?" exclaimed Sniveller.

"Yes, of course, you!" thundered McRookery. "As you've just said, we can join forces and beat the vampires – you down there, me up here!"

"But . . . I'll be scared down that dark well!" whined Sniveller.

"That's just why you must go down," growled McRookery. "So that you can conquer that silly fear of yours!"

"Silly?" exclaimed Sniveller indignantly. "If a vampire bites me on the neck, I don't think that's silly!"

"You don't believe in vampires, do you?" McRookery retorted grumpily.

"Not in the daytime, no . . ." murmured Sniveller.

"Anyway, I don't want to go in that dirty old well," he went on. "I haven't got the right clothes on!"

"Rubbish!" spat McRookery. "Your dressing-gown is just the job. Now get on with it!"

"No, I won't," retorted Sniveller.

McRookery gave a furious snort. "Does this mean you refuse?"

"No." Sniveller giggled. "I just want to fetch my grey overalls. I'll be right back."

Rapid footsteps over the gravel showed that Sniveller had wasted no time putting his words into practice.

"Wait for me, Ralph!" Tony heard McRookery's voice disappearing too.

A heavy weight seemed to fall from his shoulders. It had turned out all right just in time! Now he must get out of the well as quickly as possible, before the Nightwatchman and his assistant returned! But first he must close off the opening to the passage . . .

Tony tugged and pulled at the marble slab. At last he managed to push it across the opening. No one would find it easy to believe that behind the crumbling stone, which he was now sprinkling with a little sand to camouflage it, there was a passage. As for Sniveller, he'd have only one thought in his mind when he got down here: how to get out again as quickly as possible!

He probably wouldn't even get as far as the marble slab, but would take to his heels after one glance at the water in the well, which looked several metres deep! In fact, it hardly came up to Tony's knees.

Tony swung himself up on to the rusty iron ladder which was fixed to the walls of the well, and climbed up the narrow rungs, overgrown with moss. All the time, he was straining his ears to listen – but up in the cemetery, all was quiet. Sniveller and McRookery had probably reached their house by now, so there was no danger from them – at least for the moment.

But Greg was another matter!

Tony just hoped that Greg had run away from the Nightwatchman and his assistant. But he might easily have simply hidden behind a bush. Seeing McRookery and Sniveller's interest in the well, he might even have begun to suspect that Tony was using the old emergency exit from the vault in order to give him the slip. Greg wasn't stupid!

Tony's legs felt like jelly as he reached the top rung of the ladder. Cautiously he peered over the rim of the well, already half expecting to find himself looking straight into Greg's angry face. But there was no one to be seen, in any direction.

He climbed out of the well and, bent double, raced over to the chapel and waited a couple of minutes in the shadow of the wall. It was still possible Greg was perched up in the top of a tree. And even worse than a meeting on the ground, Tony shuddered at the thought of coming up against him in mid-air! But nothing appeared. He must have taken to his heels after all. Tony gave a sigh of relief.

Then a door slammed, and someone cursed: "Are you trying to wake up the entire cemetery?" It was McRookery!

"No!" came Sniveller's weedy reply. "The door just slipped out of my hands"

Tony ran behind the chapel. There he spread out his arms under his cloak, moved them up and down a couple of times, and flew into the air.

From a safe height, he looked down on McRookery and Sniveller. The Assistant Gardener had changed his dressing-gown for a pair of grey overalls – the same as the

Nightwatchman was wearing. But from McRookery's pockets poked large, pointed wooden stakes – at least ten of them!

Tony thought anxiously of Anna, lying all alone and ill in her coffin. But it wasn't the first time, he suddenly remembered. And vampires know that they're always in danger – in danger of their lives, if you can talk of "lives" in their case! What was more, McRookery didn't look at all as well as he made out to be. He had adopted a tired, shuffling gait after his long illness.

Sniveller was pretty harmless. After all, he had even "made friends" with Greg, when McRookery was away recuperating at his nursing home.

Feeling a little bit happier, Tony set off on the flight back to the hostel.

Flyswotter Missed You!

As he approached Crumbletomb, Tony began to forget his experiences at the cemetery. Suddenly he began to worry instead that while he'd been away, his empty bed might have been discovered.

Even when he could see the hostel and Mr Dredfel's house down below him, and realized that there were no lights at any of the windows, the feeling of unease refused to go away. Perhaps Mr Flyswotter hadn't switched on any lights on purpose, so as to "surprise" him . . .

Tony landed in the yard, behind a tree. He crept over to the dining room on tiptoe. The window was pulled to, just as he'd left it. He opened it. Nothing moved inside. Suddenly he remembered that he was still wearing the vampire cloak. He quickly pulled it off and stuffed it under his jumper. Then he climbed into the building.

He really did seem to be in luck. The passage lay deserted, the only light the glimmer of the nightlight above the washroom door. It was hard to imagine that behind all the doors, his classmates were fast asleep! Even Mr Flyswotter's door was closed.

Tony reached his dormitory without anyone seeing him. With the last of his strength, he hid the cloak in his cupboard and pulled on his pyjamas. Then he fell into bed and slept like a log.

Tony woke up because his feet felt cold. He sat up,

feeling confused, and found himself surrounded by grinning faces.

"Are you trying to sleep through till lunchtime?" asked Olly, who had pulled his covers off.

"What time is it?" muttered Tony.

"Half past eight," replied Sebastian.

"Half past eight?" Now Tony was wide awake. "So you've all had breakfast?"

Olly nodded. "You didn't miss much, though."

"Old Flyswotter missed you," Henry told him.

"Did he?"

"Yes. But we were kind and told him you were ill," answered Sebastian. "He's coming along to see you. Perhaps you'll be allowed to stay in bed, and won't have to come traipsing along to the Barren Mountains."

"The Barren Mountains?" The prospect of staying in bed instead seemed very inviting. Tony lay back on his pillows again. "You're right," he said. "I do feel rather funny. I probably overdid it a bit yesterday. In the races," he added.

"Or when you were digging up coffins," remarked Sebastian.

"Digging up coffins?" repeated Tony, startled. Did Sebastian suspect something?

"Just look at your hands," said Sebastian. "You look as though you work in a cemetery or somewhere!"

Tony went pale. His hands were quite black!

"I – I'd better go and wash them," he said, meaning to add, "before Old Flyswotter gets here."

But at that moment, the door opened and Mr Flyswotter came in, accompanied by Mrs Tallhat.

"I hear you don't feel well," he said, looking closely at Tony.

Tony had hidden his hands under the covers.

"I do feel rather odd," he said, and coughed.

Mr Flyswotter felt his forehead. "You haven't got a temperature," he announced.

"But I feel terribly tired," said Tony, which was of course quite true. "Perhaps I'm getting 'flu."

"He does seem rather pale and washed out," Mrs Tallhat put in. "I think he should stay in bed, if that's what he feels like. Sometimes a few hours' sleep works wonders."

"Hmmm . . ." muttered Mr Flyswotter. He obviously wasn't taken in quite so easily by Tony's "illness".

"Don't you think a bit of activity and fresh air would be just as good?" he asked, turning to Mrs Tallhat.

"A *little* bit of activity, maybe," agreed Mrs Tallhat. "But an hour's march there and an hour back – that's too much."

"All right then," agreed Mr Flyswotter. He wore the dissatisfied expression that he always put on at school when someone didn't hand in their maths homework and produced a letter of excuse from their parents instead. "But only till lunchtime," he said. "If you still haven't got a temperature, you'll have to get up!"

Tony nodded, careful not to let his relief and pleasure show. It was going to be a very reviving morning.

He slept until ten o'clock and enjoyed the peace of paradise. Mrs Dredfel came in once and brought him a cup of peppermint tea and two pieces of toast and marmalade. He drank the tea reluctantly, but wolfed down the toast hungrily.

His classmates came back just before one. It was obvious from the bad-tempered expressions on their faces that they hadn't particularly enjoyed the walk.

"The Barren Mountains were even less exciting than Devil's Rocks," groaned Sebastian.

"And I've ruined my smart new socks just to see them!" said Henry grimly, holding out his sports socks, which had been so clean and white before, and showing the worn out heels.

"If I'd known, I'd have stayed in bed too," said Olly, with an envious look at Tony, who was sitting happily on the edge of his bed looking completely rested. "Once again, you've been the cleverest of us all!"

Tony grinned. "I wasn't clever, I was ill!"

"So we see," growled Henry.

"What do you mean?" said Tony, all innocence. "Didn't you hear what Mrs Tallhat said: sometimes a couple of hours' sleep works wonders?"

"I could do with a couple of hours' sleep, too!" sighed Olly.

"Sleep? Right now it's time for Crumbletomb's menu of delectable delights!" teased Sebastian.

A Real Collector's Item

In fact, lunch that day wasn't too bad after all: there was home-made apple pie and pancakes.

Tony had got up for lunch, and he couldn't help noticing that Viola kept looking at him worriedly.

After the meal, when they were all out in the yard, she asked him, "Were you ill?"

"No," he answered. "Just worn out!"

"Me too!" she giggled.

Then, speaking in a whisper so that none of the others would hear, she went on, "These meetings with Rudolph are rather exhausting, aren't they?"

Tony nodded.

"But then you often hear that about actors," Viola went on. "Apparently, they demand a lot from their friends."

"You can say that again!" said Tony fervently.

'I only meant, they're such individual, special people, they're a challenge!" Viola corrected herself.

People? Tony repeated to himself, with a grin. Out loud, he said softly, "May I see the signed photograph?"

"The photograph?"

"Haven't you kept it?"

"Of course I have!" Viola told him. "But it isn't a proper photo. It's only a drawing."

"Only a drawing? That must be the printer's proof then," said Tony cunningly.

"The what?"

"The proof. Once the film is finished and going round the cinemas, Rudolph will needs hundreds – no, thousands – of signed photographs for his fans!"

"As many as that?"

"Sometimes there aren't even enough," Tony told her. "And then, of course, they stick a photo from the film on to the card – in the place where there's a drawing at the moment."

"Oh, I see," said Viola.

She glanced over at the other boys. Olly, Henry and Sebastian were watching them with unconcealed curiosity. "Does that mean my card is especially valuable?" she asked in a whisper.

"Oh yes, of course," Tony told her. That wasn't even a lie, if it was true that Greg had drawn it himself. "You could say it's a real collector's item!"

Viola smiled reflectively. "When do you think Rudolph's film will be finished? I want to know because of the world première – so I can be prepared for it."

"Oh, it's hard to say," answered Tony vaguely. "It depends on so many things . . ."

Viola ran her fingers through her hair. "If only you knew how excited I am," she sighed, gazing longingly into the distance. Then she asked, "Will Rudolph be coming tonight as well?"

"Tonight?" Tony hesitated. "I don't think he can come till tomorrow – for the farewell party!"

"Is he coming to *our* party?" exclaimed Viola loudly.

"Sssh!" Tony scolded. "Yes, probably. As long as he's finished filming for the day."

No one Can Resist You

Viola had gone quite pink with excitement and pleasure. "Are you sure the party's on?" she asked.

"Well . . ." Tony nodded his head in the direction of Mr Flyswotter, who was sitting on a bench reading his newspaper. "It probably wouldn't hurt to go and work on him a bit."

"Work on him?"

"Yes!" Tony grinned. "After all, no one can resist you!"

Viola giggled, flattered. "I don't know . . ."

"You'll do it!" said Tony slyly. "Just think what it'll be like if Rudolph *does* come to our party!"

"OK then." Viola ran her hands through her hair once more, then tripped off to the bench.

Tony sauntered over to Olly and the others.

"What does Viola want with old Flyswotter?" asked Henry.

"To ask him about the party," replied Tony. "Because she's *so* looking forward to dancing with *you* tomorrow evening!"

"Idiot!" hissed Henry, but he had gone just as pink as Viola.

"I hope she manages it," said Olly. "If we have a party, at least there'll be *one* happy memory to the holiday!"

And she did. It only took about ten minutes before Viola came back to them, eyes shining, and announced that Mr Flyswotter had agreed to the party.

How she had actually got him round to the idea, Viola kept to herself. To Henry's blunt question as to whether she had "bewitched" the maths teacher, she simply replied with a smile of contempt, "I didn't *need* to do that!"

It was only later, after tea, when she had a minute alone with Tony, that she revealed the secret. "I was going on about my class at my old school, and the great feeling we had of all belonging together – and that *our* teacher always used to say that celebrations, especially farewell parties, were one of the most important ingredients of a school trip. And then of course old Flyswotter could hardly say no!"

"Very clever of you!" remarked Tony admiringly.

"Wasn't it?" said Viola. "Now we just need to make sure Rudolph doesn't let us down. Without him, it won't be any fun at all." She looked over at the edge of the woods. "Do you think he might be waiting for us after all?"

"Now?" Tony grinned. It was still broad daylight! "I'm pretty sure he won't be coming before tomorrow evening. You know, sometimes filming goes on well into the night."

Viola nodded knowingly. "There's one thing I've been meaning to ask you," she began. "How does Rudolph actually get over here from the film set?"

Tony gave a start. "Get here?" he murmured, playing for time while he thought up a suitable explanation.

"He could hardly *fly*!" giggled Viola. "Even if they know how to do some fantastic tricks in the film . . . they wouldn't be able to fly, not really fly."

"Rudolph *does* come out of the sky," said Tony.

Viola's eyes widened. "By plane?"

"Not exactly . . ."

"In a helicopter?"

"You could call it that."

Viola shook her head in amazement. "They hire a helicopter especially, just for Rudolph to come and see you!"

"No!" Now Tony couldn't help grinning. "Just for Rudolph to come and see *you*!"

"What?" For a moment, Viola was speechless. "I don't understand . . ."

"There's nothing *to* understand," said Tony, trying hard to keep a straight face. "When you're shooting a film, you have to do all you can to keep the filmstars in a good mood. Surely you've read about that."

"Yes."

"That's why they aim to grant as many of their wishes as possible," Tony went on. "If Rudolph wants to come and see you, then they simply have to lay on a helicopter for him – so that the next day he can concentrate on the film and play his part as well as he can."

Tony held his breath. It was a pretty fantastic story he had just thought up for Viola, but because it flattered her vanity, it was just possible she would believe it.

"Rudolph flies here in a helicopter all because of me?" she asked, obviously impressed.

Tony bit his lips. "Yes. After all, no one can resist you. Especially not Rudolph!"

Viola flushed a deep red. "I don't know what to say," she whispered. Overcome, she turned away and ran off. Tony watched her until she vanished into the youth hostel. His revelation had obviously sent her into such a turmoil that she wanted to be alone for a while. That meant she must have believed his story about Rudolph needing his every wish granted. Otherwise she wouldn't have run away, but would have pestered him with more questions!

As befitted a would-be film star, Viola wasn't just vain – she also had the most vivid imagination!

People are Full of Surprises

At supper time, Viola said she thought it would be brilliant if the farewell party could have a theme.

"Oh, yes!" exclaimed Henry. "A pirate ship! Then we could all dress up as pirates!"

"And you'd be the pirate captain who gets the beautiful princess, would you?" asked Olly spitefully.

"I vote we have the Wild West!" Sebastian called out.

"Wild West? But we haven't got any cowboy hats or pistols!" said Henry disagreeably.

"But we've all got something black, haven't we?" asked Viola, looking round at everyone with a disarming smile.

Sebastian grinned. "After four days in Crumbletomb, practically everything I've got is black!"

"Well then, we'll make it a *vampire* party!" declared Viola. This seemed to hit the bull's eye – and not only with Tony.

"A vampire party? Great!" "What a good idea!" "It'll make up for the whole boring week!" These and other comments came thick and fast.

Only Mr Flyswotter wore a sour expression.

"Vampire party? That's just asking for something stupid to happen!" he said crossly.

"What sort of stupid thing?" asked Viola, looking wide-eyed and innocent.

"Well, supposing someone bites someone else?"

answered Mr Flyswotter.

Some children giggled.

"No one will bite anyone," Mrs Nutcake put in. "We once held a vampire party and it was great fun and not in the least bit bloodthirsty."

Tony looked at her in amazement. Mrs Nutcake and her daughter Kathryn, Tony's class mate, went up considerably in his estimation now he knew that they were interested in vampires! People are full of surprises, he thought.

"Hmmm!" said Mr Flyswotter. Searching for an ally, he turned to Mrs Tallhat. "What do you think about it?"

But he didn't have any luck with her either.

"If the children would enjoy it . . ." said Mrs Tallhat. "I think it's very admirable that they should develop their own ideas. And we could get a vampire party off the ground with very simple props – not like a pirate party or a cowboy party. I've already got two red lipsticks, powder and eyebrow pencil —"

"And we can go and buy the rest!" cried Kathryn. "I've hardly spent anything up till now!"

"Me neither!" "I haven't spent anything either!" came from all sides.

"The decorations wouldn't be very difficult," Mrs Nutcake went on. "All we need is red and black crêpe paper, a couple of creepy pictures on the walls . . ."

"And red juice," suggested Olly.

"And red lollies," added Sebastian.

Suddenly, everyone had an idea how to make the vampire party even more fun, and everyone started to talk at once. The result was that different working groups were set up.

Tony joined the Costume and Make-up group. As the others in the group began to discuss whether their faces should be painted white or green, he heard Viola saying to Mr Flyswotter, "You see? This is just what our old teacher meant by a sense of belonging together."

Mr Flyswotter nodded, looking as if he had just bitten on something very sour. But what could he say?

Tricks are all Part of the Business

"That was a brilliant idea of yours to think of a vampire party!" Tony told Viola later in the yard.

"It was just a trick," she replied.

"A trick?" Tony didn't understand.

"Just imagine if Rudolph was the only one dressed as a vampire tomorrow evening!" Viola giggled. "All the girls would be crowding round him! Then they'd all find out that he's an actor and right in the middle of making a vampire film – that's what I want to avoid at all costs!"

She gave a flirty sort of laugh. "Do you think I'm very mean?"

"Mean?" repeated Tony, unsure what was the best reply.

"Yes, because I want to keep Rudolph all to myself! But after all, I have to think of my career too," went on Viola in a determined voice. "If I don't build up some good connections, I'll never be famous. Anyway, tricks are all part of the business," she added with self-satisfaction. "You can read that in any film magazine."

"You won't have Rudolph *entirely* to yourself," Tony put in.

"Won't I?"

"No. Rudolph going to bring someone with him tomorrow evening."

"He's bringing someone?" said Viola, puzzled. Then a triumphant little smile appeared on her lips. "Oh, I see," she trilled. "He'll be bringing his director along too!"

Then she asked confidentially, "Do you think he'll want to do some test photographs of me straight away?"

Tony had difficulty in keeping a straight face. "Certainly not. Actually, Rudolph's bringing . . . a girl with him."

Viola's face darkened. "A girl?"

"Yes. She plays Rudolph's younger sister in the film."

"Is she Rudolph's girlfriend?"

"No," Tony assured her.

"Then why is he bringing her with him?" asked Viola crossly.

"Because Anna wants to come to such a fabulous farewell party, too," answered Tony – rather too quickly, as he immediately realized.

"Anna?" repeated Viola. "Did you just say Anna?"

Tony felt himself going red. "Yes. Why?"

"Because you've mentioned that name before . . ." Viola chewed her lip thoughtfully. "I know – on Tuesday, when I met you in the woods, just before Rudolph turned up. You turned round and said 'Anna?'!"

"Did I? I really don't remember," Tony lied.

"Yes, you did!" Viola said firmly. "I asked you who Anna was, and you said it was short for Tanya!"

"Oh, yes," Tony admitted. "It was an excuse. I didn't want you to be jealous of Anna."

Viola studied him thoughtfully. "So Anna's *your* girlfriend!" she said at last.

Tony nodded.

"That means you're going out with a real film star!" Viola's voice rang with real respect.

"Hmm, yes," said Tony.

"I'd already noticed that you didn't seem to be as boring and childish as the others," said Viola approvingly. "But it's no wonder if your girlfriend's an actress!"

Tony grinned. At that moment, he quite fancied himself as an actor!

"And did you get to know Rudolph through your girlfriend – Anna?"

"Sort of."

"What do you mean, sort of?"

"Ask Rudolph. He can explain it better than me," retorted Tony, hoping that in all the hub-bub of the farewell party, Viola wouldn't get the chance to fire questions at Rudolph. However, wasn't it Viola who had said, "Tricks are part of the business"?

"I'll do that," she said. "I've got a whole list of questions to ask him: the name of his director, what his next film will be, and, of course, when the world première will take place!" "Actually," she added, "This Anna he's bringing tomorrow, I suppose she'll be there at the world première?"

"Of course."

"And you too?"

"I'm not sure yet," said Tony evasively. "Because . . . because Anna's only playing Rudolph's younger sister."

"I see." Viola giggled. "Rudolph's got a more important part!"

"Oh yes, much more important!" said Tony with total conviction.

Viola smiled in delight, just as though Tony had said something flattering about *her*!

"It's going to be mega-brill, tomorrow evening," she sighed. "Just think – a party with two real actors . . ." And winking at Tony, she added, "And the most exciting thing is that no one apart from us two will know who they really are!"

Tony bit his tongue so as not to laugh. Only one person knew who they *really* were, and that was himself!

Rattling Sabres

That evening, Tony was in bed by nine o'clock. He was so tired that he couldn't even join in with the others' giggling and whispering. He barely heard Mr Flyswotter's furious announcement that he would have to think again about the farewell party if there wasn't absolute quiet at once in all the rooms.

It was only the next morning, when Olly started to shake him by the shoulders, that he remembered old Flyswotter's threat.

"Is the party on or not?" he asked anxiously.

"'Course it's on!" said Olly confidently. "Old Flyswotter was only rattling his sabre! Anyway, we were all quiet by half past eleven!"

"Not till half past eleven?" said Tony. If he knew Mr Flyswotter, he'd be bound to call off the party and put a forced march on instead, as a punishment!

However, either Tony had misjudged Mr Flyswotter, or the imminent end of the school trip had made him more lenient. Whatever the case, Mr Flyswotter had no complaints to make at breakfast. He didn't even want to take them on any more walks, as Tony had feared he might – a sort of farewell wander to go with the farewell party, so that they'd all be nice and tired by the evening!

That afternoon, as Tony watched Mr Flyswotter helping Mrs Nutcake's group decorate the dining room, he suddenly had the feeling that in the last few days, Mr

Flyswotter must have been playing a rôle: that of the strict teacher who wouldn't let anyone have any fun. In the same way, the Little Vampire had slipped so easily into the rôle of film star for Viola's sake . . . But we'll find out just how nice and sociable old Flyswotter really is tonight at the party! thought Tony. Especially when two strange guests suddenly appear . . .

To begin with, the party was supposed to start at seven o'clock. However, after Tony had objected that that was a totally impossible time for a vampire party, and Viola and others had joined in his protests, Mr Flyswotter agreed to put off the start until eight.

The boys began to put on their make-up at half past seven under Tony's expert guidance, of course. Viola was responsible for helping the girls with their vampire looks.

Shortly before eight, the boys had transformed themselves into more or less fiendish-looking vampires, with the help of white baby cream, baby powder, black and brown eyebrow pencil and blood-red lipstick.

They stood laughing in front of the wide mirror, comparing their faces. Olly, who had drawn jet-black rings five centimetres wide under his eyes, looked the most horrifying – but also the most unrealistic. Tony had been more subtle with his make-up, and was very pleased with the result. He wondered whether Anna would recognize him straight away among the thirteen other 'vampire' boys in the class!

They had styled their hair with colourless gel and all were wearing dark clothes. Tony had black trousers and a dark grey jumper.

The girls, who needed longer to do their make-up, looked even more "dead cool", as Mrs Nutcake put it approvingly.

Viola seemed to have a talent as a make-up artist! Tony looked rather enviously at the girls with their glittering, deep blue eyelids, greenish-white skin and artistically tousled hair.

Mrs Tallhat and Mrs Nutcake were also made up to look like vampires and were wearing black. Only Mr Flyswotter came down in his usual baggy cord trousers and a checked shirt.

"That won't do at all, Mr Flyswotter," Mrs Nutcake scolded him – she was obviously feeling rather daring in her vampire costume. "You *must* get dressed up too!"

"Yes, you must!" agreed Mrs Tallhat gaily. "Otherwise you'll find yourself being bitten by vampires!"

Mr Flyswotter gave an embarrassed grin. "Do you think so?"

"If you're the only human among all these vampires . . .' replied Mrs Tallhat.

"I don't know how to put on make-up, though," Mr Flyswotter said defensively.

"Oh, I'll help you," offered Viola.

"I don't know, I just don't know." Mr Flyswotter tried to refuse.

"Come on!" said Mrs Nutcake firmly. "Viola and I will transform you into a proper vampire."

"If you think you can . . ." chuckled Mr Flyswotter.

What's the Time, Count Dracula?

And they did. When Mr Flyswotter reappeared ten minutes later, he was hardly recognizable. His face was covered in a greenish-white layer of cream and powder, his hair stood up wildly all over his head, and his eyes looked enormous, circled with thick black lines. He was wearing a dark brown shirt and black trousers.

Henry ran over to the music system. He had borrowed it from one of the church groups – the youth hostel only had an ancient gramophone, which was broken!

What was more, the people in the church office had also given him a box of good rock'n'roll records.

"I declare the vampire party open!" announced Henry, adding with a grin, "Mr Flyswotter and Mrs Nutcake will take the floor for the first dance!"

The opening bars of a mind-blowing rock'n'roll record rang out. Mr Flyswotter made a face as if he had toothache. But Mrs Nutcake took him firmly by the arm and pulled him to the middle of the floor.

"On with the vampire ball!" she laughed.

Mr Flyswotter shrugged his shoulders as if resigned to his fate, and began to jerk and swing his legs and arms in a most extraordinary way. Some of the children giggled, but only behind their hands.

Tony saw Olly go up to Viola and bow. With a sweet smile, she followed him on to the dance floor.

Henry, who was standing by the music system,

watched them with a darkening expression on his face. When the record came to an end, he switched off the record player and called, "That's that for now. We'll have some games instead."

"Hey, *you* can't be the one to decide that!" complained Tanya, and Sonia added angrily, "It's not your party, after all!"

"But I *am* responsible for the music system," Henry told them loftily, "and I can decide when the record player needs a break!"

"The only one who needs a break round here is you!" said Tanya crossly.

"If you mean . . ." said Henry calmly. "But then you won't have any music at all. The guy in the church office said no one was to use the equipment except me!"

"Well, let's all start with some games," Mr Flyswotter put in. He was probably rather glad that he didn't have to dance any more!

"Games!" grumbled Sonia.

"Just wait and see what we've got in store for you!" Mrs Nutcake said, trying to keep the peace. "Gripping vampire games!"

"Vampire games?" thought Tony sceptically.

He was right. They were only well-known and rather boring games which Mrs Nutcake had given new names to. "Pass the Parcel" had turned into "Unwrap the Corpse", "Blind Man's Buff " became "Blind Bat's Buff " and "What's the Time, Mr Wolf?" became "What's the Time, Count Dracula?"

How stunningly original! Tony sighed. Even "Musical Chairs" – that stupid game where you run round a circle of chairs and scramble for a free one when the music stops – wasn't any more exciting when it was called "Musical Funerals", with every chair supposedly an empty coffin! So Tony didn't bother to find himself an empty chair, and by the second round, he was out. Viola followed his example.

When is Rudolph Coming?

"When do you think Rudolph will come?" Viola asked in a whisper, as soon as she could get near Tony. Tony was watching in amusement as the others ran round the chairs as though their lives depended on it. Even Henry was kept busy switching the music on and off. All he could do was glare at Tony and Viola.

"When will he come? Not for a while, I think," said Tony.

"But my hair's a mess now!" wailed Viola. She tried to push it back into place with her hands. "It's such a nuisance that we didn't have any hairspray!"

"Don't worry," said Tony. "Rudolph hates hairspray."

"Really?"

"Sure. First, because it stinks. And secondly, because he's concerned about the hole in the ozone layer."

"What's Rudolph got to do with the ozone layer?"

"Nothing. But he hates sunlight."

"Oh, I see . . ." Viola looked as though she didn't. She glanced across at the window.

"Perhaps he's waiting for us outside?"

"No, I'm sure he's not," said Tony.

"How do you know?" asked Viola.

Tony only just stopped himself from grinning. "Because they go on filming till it gets dark. They only stop when the sun goes down."

"And then they'll come straight here?"

"I suppose so, yes."

"In the helicopter?"

Now Tony couldn't stop himself. "Yes," he said with a grin. "In their private helicopter!"

"Then we'll be able to hear it!" remarked Viola. "Helicopters are very loud."

"True," Tony admitted. "But they'll land outside the village."

"Even further out than we are here?" asked Viola with a giggle.

"Yes – they don't want to wake anyone up in the youth hostel."

Viola gave a start. "You mean, they won't come until we've all gone to bed?"

"No, today they'll be here earlier," Tony assured her. Then, with a glance up at the night sky, he added, "As soon as possible, I hope!"

"Then I'd better not dance any more," murmured Viola. "Otherwise my hair will be totally ruined by the time Rudolph arrives. You do understand, don't you?" she asked flatteringly.

"Me? Of course!" In fact Tony had no intention of dancing with Viola!

In any case, there wasn't any dancing for the moment. Following on from "Musical Funerals" came a game called "Pairs of Pointed Fangs". It sounded very promising, but in fact was nothing more than a different name for the tried and tested guessing game, "Double Meanings".

"Take the word 'fiddle'," began Mrs Nutcake with a serious expression. "On the one hand, you're talking about a musical instrument like a violin. On the other hand, there's a different kind of fiddle —"

"Yes, a swindle or a cheat – the sort of thing Tony

Peasbody's so good at!" cried Henry, who was cross because Viola had sat down next to Tony.

Tony just grinned.

"You shouldn't tease Henry," he whispered to Viola. "We may need him when Rudolph and Anna arrive."

"Henry?" she asked, baffled.

"Yes. If anyone starts asking where the pair of them have come from, Henry can say they're members of the church group he borrowed the music system from."

Viola nodded in agreement. "You think of everything!" Then she went across and sat down on the empty chair next to Henry.

Hello, Tony!

After the guessing game, Mrs Tallhat announced the Vampire Feast. There wasn't as much choice as there had been at the meal Sniveller had produced – back when McRookery the Nightwatchman had been laid up in hospital and his assistant gardener had held a secret vampire fancy dress party. However, Mrs Tallhat and her group had put a lot of effort into it. The table was covered with red crêpe paper and there were red jellies and mousses, red juice and red ice lollies. The rest was ordinary – scrumptious – party food, but it was set out in longish cardboard boxes, covered with black paper to look like miniature coffins. While Tony was gazing at these "mini coffins" filled with crisps, peanuts and popcorn, someone poked him gently in the back and he heard Anna's voice saying, "How pretty it looks!"

Deliberately slowly, so as to avoid any stir, Tony turned round. There was Anna, smiling at him.

"Hallo," he said, rather embarrassed.

"Hallo, Tony," she replied sweetly.

"How did you recognize me?" he asked.

She giggled. "I'd always recognize you – even when you've put on such a brilliant disguise!" she told him.

"It's a really great party you've got here," she went on. "You never told me you were all coming as vampires!"

Tony glanced anxiously to either side, but no one was paying any attention to Anna. It was probably because with her black cloak, her shoulder-length, tousled hair and her pale face, she looked no different from the other "vampires".

"It was Viola's idea," explained Tony. "She wanted you both to be able to join in without being too noticeable."

Anna smiled mischievously. "Both of us?"

"Well, Rudolph particularly, of course," admitted Tony. "But I've told Viola about you – and that you're my girlfriend," he added.

"You told her that?" Anna sounded very pleased.

"Yes." Tony felt himself going red. "What about your hand?" he asked quickly. "Does it still hurt?"

Anna looked at her bandage and nodded. "Yes."

They had moved away from the food table, and were now standing near the widow. No one was taking any notice of them, not even Mr Flyswotter, who had just filled a plate to the brim with nuts and breadsticks.

"I'd really love to be in your class . . ." said Anna with a wistful smile.

"Yes, perhaps you would, this evening," retorted Tony. "But the last few days haven't been very pleasant!"

"Even so, I envy you," whispered Anna.

"Envy me?' said Tony, only pretending to be indignant, because Anna was suddenly looking rather sad. "If you only knew how exhausting this school trip has been! I've got thirteen blisters, seven corns and thirty-four midge bites!" That was a huge exaggeration, but perhaps it would help to cheer Anna up.

"Where?" asked Anna.

"Where? On my feet!" he said.

"Can't you dance, then?" She looked disappointed. "I've been so looking forward to it!"

"Oh yes, I'll be able to dance," Tony told her hastily. "A couple of times, anyway," he added, to be on the safe side.

"I can't dance for very long, either," Anna admitted. "Otherwise I begin to get dizzy. You know, I had to stop and land three times during our flight here!"

"Three times?"

"Yes!" Anna sniffled.

"Is that why you're looking so sad?" asked Tony cautiously.

Anna shook her head. "No. I've been watching you all from outside, that's why I'm sad."

"You've been watching us?" said Tony, with an uneasy feeling. He tried to remember whether he'd done anything which could have upset Anna. But he hadn't even had a dance yet!

"You were all sitting round in a circle," Anna told him. "First of all, you looked as if you were thinking hard. Then someone called out something, and you all laughed. It looked so . . . such fun. You were laughing, too!"

She turned her head away. "And then I suddenly thought: you and the others, you're only vampires for this evening – and only because you think it's fun. But I've got to stay like this forever, whether I like it or not!"

She gulped, and before Tony could do anything to stop her, she ran to the door. Tony hurried after her, almost bumping into Mr Flyswotter, who had just filled his plate for a second time with crisps and nuts.

Friends Never Say 'If Only...'

Tony arrived in the yard quite out of breath. Anna was nowhere to be seen. She couldn't have flown away as quickly as that – she *mustn't* have!

"Anna?" called Tony. Perhaps she'd hidden over by the trees.

Now he heard a muffled sob and ran in the direction it was coming from. He found Anna under a big old tree. She was sitting hunched up on the ground, and had pulled her cloak over her head so that nothing but the tip of her nose could be seen.

Tony came to a standstill in front of her. "Anna!" he said. "You mustn't be so sad!"

"Why not?" she asked.

"Because I like you just the way you are!" he replied.

"And *you* mustn't tell lies!"

"Lies? That's the truth!"

Anna gulped. "You would like me much more if only I *wasn't* a vampire!"

"No, I wouldn't!" Tony denied it hotly. "Friends never say 'if only'! Each person likes the other just the way they are!"

"Really?" Anna peeped out from under the cloak. "What if you'd met me back in Transylvania, when I was still a normal human girl? Don't you think you'd have liked me better then?"

"No," he said firmly. "For a start, I don't particularly

like normal girls. And secondly, I like you exactly as you are."

"Oh, Tony!" She stood up rather unsteadily. "You do say the nicest things."

"Anyhow," went on Tony, "I think something else is making you sad."

"Something else?"

"Yes. Because today you saw all my school friends for the first time."

"Mmm, you could be right," Anna said thoughtfully. "Especially all the girls in your class," she added after a pause. "They're allowed to wear whatever they want: jeans and pretty shirts and jumpers and skirts and leggings – all the latest fashions."

She pushed back her cloak so that Tony could see her dark blue velvet dress. It was trimmed with gold lace at the neck and round the hem, and Anna had tied a wide belt of gold embroidered material round her waist. "Vampire girls look so old-fashioned when they try to look nice."

"I like your dress," Tony told her.

"Really?"

"Yes. It suits the colour of your hair and your skin." Tony gave an embarrassed cough. He wasn't very good at paying compliments!

"But it isn't the latest fashion," declared Anna. "I dread to think what the girls in your class would say about it!"

"They'll think it's great!" Tony assured her.

"Yes, tonight maybe," said Anna, "because they're holding a vampire party. But by tomorrow, when everything's back to normal, they'd be pointing at me and laughing."

"But the party's tonight," said Tony. "And tomorrow they won't be lucky enough to see you!"

Anna looked at him doubtfully. "Lucky?"

"Oh, yes," said Tony. "I'm the only one who'll be lucky – if you'll come and visit me tomorrow evening back at home."

Anna smiled. "Haven't you just told me that friends never say 'if only'? Of course I'll come! And now we should be getting back," she went on. "I'll show you that I'm a match for all the other girls – and I want to dance too!" With that, she linked arms lovingly with Tony.

Squeak, Batty, Squeak!

"By the way," asked Tony, trying to sound casual as they walked across the yard, "did Rudolph come with you?"

"He did," said Anna. "But if I were you, I'd forget him."

"Forget him?" repeated Tony, puzzled.

Anna giggled. "Only for today, of course. You see, Rudolph got out of his coffin the wrong side tonight."

"What does that mean?"

"Only that sometimes he can behave even more disgracefully than Greg does."

"Greg?" Tony thought of their meeting at the cemetery with growing unease. "Greg isn't here too, is he?" he asked, looking around anxiously.

"No, no," Anna reassured him. "He's gone to his Men's Music Club." She gave another giggle. "Just imagine: Wally the Wicked is trying to fix up a tour for them!"

"A tour?"

"Yes. I don't believe it," said Anna. "But Greg's convinced that they can make a brilliant career out of it. They've even given themselves a name. They're now called 'The Swinging Vault Groovers'!" Anna laughed delightedly.

"But what's happened to *your* music?" she asked after a pause. "I can't hear anything!"

"They're probably still playing games," said Tony.

"But then Rudolph wouldn't have gone into the hostel."

"Has he gone in already?"

"Yes, at least five minutes ago."

By now they had reached the door. The sounds of voices and laughter came out to them, but no music. Had Henry given up on the music system in a fit of "disc jockey pique"?

"Here, we'll take a look from outside first," said Anna, pulling Tony along with her.

Through the window, they could see that everyone was still playing games: right now, it was obviously "Squeak, Piggy, Squeak!" because everyone – except for the Little Vampire, who was nowhere to be seen – was sitting in a circle. Tanya's eyes were blindfolded, and she was going round sitting on different children's laps while they made loud squeaking noises.

Tony didn't know what name Mrs Nutcake could have given this game. "Squeak, Batty, Squeak!" he remarked to Anna with a smile.

"What?" hissed Anna. "I'm *not* a bat! And I hate it when people call me that!"

"I didn't mean *you*," said Tony, startled at how cross she was. "Just the game."

"Did you think I didn't recognize the game?" Anna retorted crossly. "We played it on my Vampire Day, but it was called something else."

"Yes, 'Squeak, Piggy, Squeak'. That's why I changed it to 'Squeak, Batty —' "

"Squeak!" Tony was interrupted by a husky voice.

He turned his head and caught sight of the Little Vampire.

"I . . . I thought you'd gone inside," stammered Tony.

"Yes. But I don't want to play these childish games!"

replied the Little Vampire haughtily. "So I came flying out of a window again – whoosh! But first I picked up this nice little book, which someone seemed to have thrown away!" Grinning maliciously, he brought out a book bound in black, which had been hidden under his cloak.

"Hey!" cried Tony. "That's my book, *The Vampire from Amsterdam*!"

"Is it?" The vampire pretended to be amazed. "I thought it looked familiar, when I spotted it lying in the wastepaper basket. . ."

"In the wastepaper basket?" asked Tony indignantly. "It was by my bed, on a chair!"

"Oh, then it must have sprouted wings!" sniggered the Little Vampire, adding in a deep, cavernous voice, "I swear to you by Count Dracula, it was in the wastepaper basket!"

"Probably because you'd just thrown it in there!" growled Tony.

The Little Vampire said nothing, but calmly slipped the book back under his cloak. Then he drew himself up and peered into the dining room.

Anna tugged at Tony's sleeve. "Don't annoy him!" she whispered. "I'll take the book off him as soon as I get the chance!"

At that moment, the Little Vampire let out a cry – a cry of joy, as Tony quickly realized.

"Viola!" sighed the vampire, pressing his hands flat against the window pane.

Now Anna and Tony could also see that Viola had appeared at the window and was waving energetically to Rudolph.

"Oh, Viola!" said the Little Vampire. "I didn't really want to come. But when you smile at me like that . . ."

And he drifted off towards the door like a sleepwalker.

Tony was wondering whether he ought to stop the Little Vampire, when suddenly a roll of drums came from the dining room. It was the opening of a rock'n'roll hit with a loud, rhythmic beat. Surely the Little Vampire wouldn't be noticed now in the pushing, whirling crowd!

Rock Around the Clock

"What are you waiting for?" asked Anna impatiently. "I thought you said we were going to dance."

"Yes, yes," said Tony hastily. "I . . . I was just thinking about something else."

Anna looked sulky. "Viola, I suppose?"

"No!" Tony grinned. This time he could answer "Rudolph" without worrying about whether she would be jealous!

Anna giggled. "At first, Rudolph didn't want to come along at all," she told him. "I had to spend half an eternity persuading him. He said he'd been very disappointed in Viola."

"Disappointed?" Tony couldn't believe it.

"Yes. And then he just has to see her through the window and he's completely hooked again! But that's typical Rudolph – as changeable as the moon!"

Tony gave a start. "Do you mean he's growing into a teenager, like Greg?"

"Oh, Tony!" Anna nudged him teasingly. "You know that can't happen! He'll always stay the age he was when he — " She stopped. "Let's go," she said to change the subject. Then she began to sing, "Let's rock around the clock tonight!"

"Around the clock?" repeated Tony. "I bet you Mr Flyswotter will stop the party within the hour!"

"All the more reason to hurry up then!" urged Anna,

taking his arm.

When they walked into the dining room, it certainly didn't look as though the party would be over soon. Mr Flyswotter was dancing with Mrs Nutcake, and his face looked young and flushed with enjoyment.

"Is your teacher better then?" asked Anna, nodding her head towards Mrs Nutcake.

"That's not our teacher, that's Kathryn's mum," Tony explained. "She's just come along to give Mr Flyswotter some support. So has Mrs Tallhat. She's over there at the table."

"I imagine it's pretty exhausting coming along on a school trip with a horde like this!" Anna remarked.

"Horde?" Tony pretended to be indignant.

"Well . . . " Anna giggled. "The grownups always have to take responsibility for everything. And your classmates don't exactly look angelic!"

Tony grinned. "You're wrong," he said. "We're the nicest, quietest, most harmless class you could imagine!"

"If you believe that . . . " Anna smiled mischievously. She put her uninjured arm round Tony and pushed him gently on to the dance floor. Tony felt as if dozens of curious eyes were looking at them.

But it was only his imagination. Henry had just put on a new record and nearly everyone was singing along at the top of their voices, "Come on, let's twist again . . . " and trying to do the movements that went with the words: twisting down with knees bent, then up again, swivelling their hips.

Suddenly Tony caught sight of the Little Vampire. It wasn't easy to pick him out among all the "vampires", especially since he was doing everything exactly the same as everyone else – probably to impress Viola. The Little Vampire swung his hips, bent his knees and twisted right down to the floor, then came back up again, bright red in the face!

Tony bit his tongue to stop himself laughing.

"What sort of dance is this?" asked Anna.

"The twist," replied Tony.

"I don't like this dance," said Anna. "I'd rather dance with you properly."

"Properly?"

"Yes! Like we did at the Vampire Ball in the Vale of Doom. You put one hand on my waist, and I held on to your shoulder. Now *that's* a nice way to dance!"

"But people don't dance like that any more." Tony pointed to the Little Vampire and Viola, who never once touched each other. "No one dances close together. Only in ballroom dancing."

Anna pressed closer to him. "Then let's do a . . . ballroom dance!"

Tony coughed with embarrassment. "You only do that when it's a special ballroom dance evening and *everyone*'s doing it!" he said.

"Mr Flyswotter's dancing close to his partner!" Anna told him. Tony followed her gaze, and sure enough, there was Mr Flyswotter dancing the foxtrot with Mrs Tallhat.

"They're allowed to do it," he explained. "But I'd prefer not to attract attention – for your sake, so no one gets suspicious."

"And anyway," he added, seeing Anna's crestfallen expression, "We could do a ballroom dance *tomorrow*, when you come to my house – just you and me!"

Anna's eyes brightened. "Oh, yes!" she said. "I'll bring a couple of candles with me, and some of Aunt Dorothy's joss sticks, and then we can have a really cosy ballroom dance session all to ourselves!"

With that, she began cautiously imitating the movements of the other dancers: bending her knees, standing up again and twisting her hips. But after only a short time, she whispered, "I'm getting dizzy, Tony."

"Then we'd better go and sit down," said Tony worriedly. He took Anna's hand and led her to a table near one of the open windows. He hoped the cool night air would help her feel better.

"I'm sorry," she said. "Now I've spoiled the party for you."

"You? No!" Tony assured her.

"If you want to dance with someone else . . . " She blinked.

Tony shook his head firmly. "Why should I? No, I'll stay here with you." He was about to add, "I could get you something to eat," but stopped himself just in time from making this rather tactless remark to Anna!

Not with Vampires!

"Well, now! Here's a nice quiet table," said the Little Vampire in a husky voice.

Tony watched as Rudolph and Viola came and sat down a couple of tables away. The Little Vampire nodded at him and grinned.

"You really have found a nice place for us to sit, Rudolph," said Viola. "Now we can talk in peace!" She winked at Tony and took a good look at Anna, whom she had not yet met, smiling approvingly.

"What do you want to talk about?" asked the Little Vampire. His voice sounded rather wary, and not as lovesick as before, Tony thought.

"About us," murmured Viola.

"Us?" exclaimed the Little Vampire throatily. "Don't you want to talk about the film, then?"

"Oh, yes I do!" Viola said. "I want to talk about us – and especially about when we'll be able to work together in front of the camera!"

She giggled. "Don't you think I make a brilliantly good vampire this evening?"

"Yeah, yeah," growled the Little Vampire.

"What?" cried Viola. "I took a whole hour to do my hair and all you can say is, 'yeah, yeah'?"

Rudolph didn't reply. From the corner of his eye, Tony could see a dark expression settling on his face.

"What's more," went on Viola reproachfully. "I'd

been counting on you bringing along your director this evening, not just the girl who plays your little sister in the film." She smiled at Anna again.

"Oh? Why's that?" hissed the Little Vampire.

"Is it so hard to understand?" trilled Viola. "It would have been *just* the opportunity for an informal meeting! And your director could have seen how good I look in a vampire costume – or isn't his next film about vampires?" she added, as though this thought had just occurred to her.

"You just said you wanted to talk 'about us' and not about the film!" the Little Vampire complained.

"But, Rudolph," Viola tried to laugh, "you and the vampire film are one and the same thing!"

"Certainly not!" retorted the Little Vampire.

"What do you mean?" she asked.

"You only like me because I'm an actor," declared the Little Vampire.

Viola giggled. "So?" she said. "That's how it is with actors."

"Maybe," answered Rudolph in a hollow voice, "but not with vampires!"

With these words, he stood up. He gave Tony another gloomy look, as if he could do something about the fact that Viola was only interested in Rudolph Sackville-Bagg the film star. Then he climbed up on to the window-sill and vanished into the darkness.

"R-Rudolph — " stammered Viola.

"I'd better fly after him," whispered Anna. "See you tomorrow, Tony." She got up and left the room in the same way as the Little Vampire.

The Party's Over

"Those two are rather touchy!" Viola laughed, not at all bothered. She had sat down in Anna's place. "But that's always the way with actors." Then she asked confidentially, "I expect they had a particularly tiring day filming, did they?"

"Yes," said Tony absent-mindedly. He would have liked to have fetched his vampire cloak and followed Anna and Rudolph. . .

"It's what happens when a film's nearly finished," boasted Viola with her expert knowledge. "Everyone gets over-tense."

Tony didn't reply.

"Shall we dance?" she asked.

"No, now it's *my* turn!" interrupted Henry, bobbing up unexpectedly behind Viola.

With a bored expression, Viola looked over at the music system, which Olly seemed to be working now. "What about the record player?" she asked pointedly. "Didn't the church group say that *no one* apart from you was supposed to work it?"

"Yes." Henry grinned. "But they were talking about ordinary parties. At a *vampire* party, it's OK to let someone else take over for a while!"

"Vampire party?" said Viola scornfully, looking over at the window. "Just don't flatter yourselves. . ." And with a condescending smile, she pranced off on to the dance floor.

Tony went over to the window and looked out. Thick clouds covered the moon. He hoped Anna would manage the flight home with her injured hand. . .

Suddenly he felt someone touching his sleeve from behind.

"Anna?" he said in surprise. But it was only Viola.

"I just left him there," she announced. "That Henry's a real pain in the neck!"

"Not only Henry!" sighed Tony.

"Let's dance!" begged Viola.

But at that moment, Mr Flyswotter called out, "Right! The party's over!"

"Typical!" sniffed Viola. "Just when it's getting going, it's time to stop!"

"Stop?" Tony thought of the following evening. "No, it won't be stopping for a while!" And as Viola gazed at him, puzzled, he walked out of the door.

In the bus the next morning everyone agreed that the class trip had been quite fun after all.

"We never thought you could be so nice," said Mary to Mr Flyswotter.

He gave an embarrassed cough. "I could say the same about you lot."

Tony's mother was waiting for him when the bus got back. "Well?" she inquired. "Have you all had a good trip?"

"The last evening was brilliant!" Olly told her. "We had a vampire party!"

"A vampire party?" she repeated, not particularly enthusiastically. "I bet that was Tony's idea!"

"What makes you think that?" retorted Tony.

"It was Viola's idea, actually," Olly assured her.

"You see?" said Tony with a grin. "Other people occasionally get good ideas too!" With that, he climbed happily into the car.

Find out what happens to Tony and his vampire friends in the next book in this series, *The Little Vampire and the Christmas Surprise*.

THE LITTLE VAMPIRE series

Watch out for new titles in the spooky *Little Vampire* series:

Book 1: **The Little Vampire in Danger**
Book 2: **The Little Vampire in the Vale of Doom**
Book 3: **The Little Vampire in Despair**
Book 4: **The Little Vampire and the Mystery Patient**
Book 5: **The Little Vampire in the Lion's Den**
Book 6: **The Little Vampire Learns to be Brave**
Book 7: **The Little Vampire Gets a Surprise**
Book 8: **The Little Vampire and the Wicked Plot**
Book 9: **The Little Vampire and the School Trip**

And look out for these new books:

Book 10: **The Little Vampire and the Christmas Surprise**
Book 11: **The Little Vampire at Count Dracula's Castle**